Chiara Lubich
Essential Teachings on Unity

MODERN SPIRITUAL MASTERS SERIES

CHIARA LUBICH
Essential Teachings on Unity

Edited by
PETER CASARELLA AND THOMAS MASTERS

Maryknoll, New York 10545

Orbis Books, the publishing arm of the Maryknoll Fathers and Brothers, endeavors to publish works that enlighten the mind, nourish the spirit, and challenge the conscience. To learn more about Maryknoll and Orbis Books, please visit our website at www.orbisbooks.com.

Copyright © 2026 by Peter Casarella and Thomas Masters

Published by Orbis Books, Box 302, Maryknoll, NY 10545-0302.

All rights reserved.

Excerpts from the published writings of Chiara Lubich are used with permission from Focolare Media/New City Press, 360 N Pacific Coast Hwy Suite 2000, El Segundo, CA 90245. Unpublished writings are used with permission from Archivio Generale Movimento Focolare, Archivio Chiara Lubich, and the Focolare Office for Wisdom and Study, Via di Frascati, 306, 00040 Rocca di Papa (Roma), Italy.

Cover photo published with the permission of Centro S. Chiara Audiovisivi s.r.l., Rocca di Papa—Via Castelli Romani, 89 (Italy).

Scripture quotations are from New Revised Standard Version Bible, copyright © 1989, National Council of the Churches of Christ in the United States of America. Used by permission. All rights reserved worldwide.

No part of this publication may be reproduced or transmitted in any form or by any means, electronic or mechanical, including photocopying, recording, or any information storage or retrieval system, without prior permission in writing from the publisher.

Queries regarding rights and permissions should be addressed to: Orbis Books, P.O. Box 302, Maryknoll, NY 10545-0302.

Manufactured in the United States of America

Library of Congress Cataloging-in-Publication Data
Names: Lubich, Chiara, 1920-2008 author | Casarella, Peter J. editor | Masters, Thomas, 1947- editor
Title: Essential writings on unity / Chiara Lubich ; edited by Peter Casarella and Thomas Masters.
Description: Maryknoll, NY : Orbis Books, [2026] | Series: Modern spiritual masters | Includes bibliographical references.
Identifiers: LCCN 2025032587 (print) | LCCN 2025032588 (ebook) | ISBN 9781626986497 trade paperback | ISBN 9798888661031 epub
Subjects: LCSH: Church—Unity | Spirituality—Catholic Church | Catholic Church—Doctrines
Classification: LCC BV601.5 .L83 2026 (print) | LCC BV601.5 (ebook)
LC record available at https://lccn.loc.gov/2025032587
LC ebook record available at https://lccn.loc.gov/2025032588

Contents

FOREWORD
Sarah Coakley — vii

CHIARA LUBICH: LIVING WITNESS TO A CHARISM OF UNITY
Peter Casarella — xvii

TIMELINE OF SIGNIFICANT EVENTS — xxxv

1. ORIGINS AND TRAJECTORIES — 1
   Introduction — 1
   Chiara Lubich: Family and Childhood — 2
   Lubich's First Sense of Being Called — 2
   Lubich's Education and Career as a Teacher — 3
   Intuitions at the House of Loreto — 5
   The Beginnings — 7
   The First Focolare House — 8
   Paradise '49: Chiara Lubich's Collective
     Mystical Experience — 10
   Resurrection of Rome — 16
   Foundation of the Gen Movement — 21
   The Family Is Our Future — 25
   Toward a New Humanity — 29

2. GOING TO GOD TOGETHER — 38
   Introduction — 38
   I Know Only Christ and Christ Crucified — 39
   Living the Gospel — 52
   Mary Desolate — 57
   The Eucharist and the Transformation
     of the Cosmos — 61

3. **Spirituality of Communion—Living Jesus Within**   63
   Introduction   63
   Aspects for Ordering Daily Life and Activities   63
   Like a Rainbow   68
   Becoming Saints as Church   70
   The Holy Spirit   72
   Detachment   74
   You Are Everything; I Am Nothing   79
   The Attraction of Modern Times: A Poem
      by Chiara Lubich   80
   A New Way of Life   81
   "A Spirituality for Dialogues"   86
   The Four Nights   95

4. **Spirituality of Communion—Living Jesus in Relationships**   103
   Introduction   103
   The Four Dialogues   104
   Chiara Lubich: "I Have a Dream for
      the New Millennium"   108
   The Charism of Unity and Philosophy   110
   The Charism of Unity and Theology   118
   The Charism of Unity and Education   125
   The Charism of Unity and Communications   133
   Toward an Economy of Communion   140
   The Charism of Unity and Psychology   144
   The Movement for Unity in Politics   150
   Unity with Other Christians   162
   The Focolare Movement's Experience
      of Interreligious Dialogue   172
   The Abba School   177

Bibliography   179
   Sources
   For Further Reading   180

Foreword

Sarah Coakley

I am greatly honored, and also humbled, as an Anglican woman priest and theologian to be invited to write a short foreword to this new, select collection of the writings of Chiara Lubich (1920–2008), a modern "mystic" and founder of the Focolare ("hearth") movement in Italy and worldwide.

Peter Casarella's "Introduction," which follows, will supply a rich background to Chiara Lubich's extraordinary life and witness for those not already familiar with it.[1] What I wish to add here, therefore, is only a short commendation based on three considerations that have become especially vivid for me as I have immersed myself in Lubich's writing and thinking for the first time in recent months. Each of these points of reflection is one where the distinctive *uniqueness* of Lubich's spiritual insights intersects with ongoing contemporary concerns and crises, both political and personal. And each of them, too, revolves around the particular radicality of Lubich's teaching on "unity," the special focus of this collection of her writings.

---

1. Along with the selections from Lubich's writings chosen for this little volume, I am also drawing here gratefully on the more expansive collection, Chiara Lubich, *Essential Writings: Spirituality, Dialogue, Culture*, ed. Michael Vandeleene (London: New City Press, 2007); Rowan Williams's "Introduction" (xiii–ix) to that volume; and Piero Coda's "The Spirituality of Unity in the Christian Vocation" (xxi–xxx).

"Feminine Spirituality" or Reoriented Humanity?

It might be tempting, first, to allocate Chiara Lubich's mystical insights to the category of "feminine spirituality," a term that has much exercised modern theological scholarship, whether in denigration or approbation. An older tradition of male scholarship and spiritual direction (the great abbot John Chapman, OSB, comes to mind[2]) notoriously homogenized all "female mysticism" as affective, anti-intellectual, and therefore intrinsically inferior to its male counterpart; whereas the transformative feminist historical scholarship of the later twentieth century recaptured the theological significance and distinctiveness of women's mystical experiences and teaching throughout Christianity, and especially in the medieval period and on into the early modern tradition.[3] Harder to clarify has been the extent to which the outstanding voices of Catholic women saints and mystics have (inevitably) been both *promulgated* by men and, to some extent, adjusted by the officialdom of the Church to accommodate their teaching and examples to more famil-

---

2. John Chapman, OSB, "Mysticism (Roman Catholic)," in *Encyclopaedia of Religion and Ethics*, ed. J. Hastings (Edinburgh: T&T Clark, 1908–26). I comment on this important article and its extraordinary denigration of "female mysticism" in Sarah Coakley, *Powers and Submissions: Spirituality, Philosophy and Gender* (Oxford: Blackwell, 2002), esp. 52–53.

3. The ground-breaking academic work of Caroline Walker Bynum was crucial here from the 1970s onward: see esp. her *Jesus as Mother: Studies in the Spirituality of the High Middle Ages* (Berkeley: University of California Press, 1982), and *Holy Feast and Holy Fast: The Religious Significance of Food to Medieval Women* (Berkeley: University of California Press, 1987); and for Teresa of Ávila, Alison Weber's feminist assessment in *Teresa of Ávila and the Rhetoric of Femininity* (Princeton, NJ: Princeton University Press, 1990) remains indispensable reading.

iar or orthodox prototypes.[4] This complex historical backcloth makes our understanding of the importance of Chiara Lubich's distinctive witness both poignant and explosive. At times, her writing may remind us—as I was myself reminded, on first reading her—of striking earlier visionaries and mystical theologians: of Lady Richeldis's original Marian vision at Walsingham, with its parallels to the Loretto Marian tradition; of the vibrant spiritual examples of humility in Francis and Clare (whose name, "Chiara," Silvia Lubich chose to take); of the extraordinary cosmic perceptions of Julian of Norwich of our created "littleness" and yet our unique incarnational significance; of Catherine of Siena's devotion to the poor and her political influence; of the "annihilative" rhetoric of John of the Cross's accounts of the dark nights and of union; of the sacrificial "little way" of Thérèse de Lisieux; and of the theme of inner-trinitarian incorporation in Elizabeth of the Trinity. All these seemingly find echoes in Lubich's work; but it is not clear whether there is any *direct* influence, as opposed to a confluence of themes that authentically spring from Lubich's own entry into the depths of Christ's passion and its immediate impact there from of the work of the Spirit. Here, arguably more significantly than in these other forebears, is the theological pincer movement that is itself at the heart of Lubich's own distinctive teaching on universal "unity."

---

4. John W. Coakley, *Women, Men and Spiritual Power: Female Saints and Their Male Collaborators* (New York: Columbia University Press, 2006), working in Bynum's train, demonstrates, with subtle attention to shifts of ecclesiastical power, how the marks of female sanctity were slowly transformed and restricted by male management and promulgation in the period between Hildegard of Bingen and Catherine of Siena.

What does this tell us, then, about Chiara Lubich as a lay woman mystic, and indeed about her importance for contemporary agonies and anxieties about gender and identity?

There are times, to be sure, when Lubich's discussion of family and gender explicitly evokes influence from Bishop Klaus Hemmerle (and behind him, his mentor, Hans Urs von Balthasar) and suggests a modern "complementarian" account of gender roles.[5] This is hardly surprising, given the tenor of her own times within Roman Catholicism, and especially the important teaching of John Paul II on the "dignity of women"—as both "equal" but essentially *different* in "genius."[6] But I venture to say here that Lubich's radical views on "unity" (at least as I read her) implicitly push beyond the presumption of gendered "complementarity" to a profounder and more challenging position. For in much of her writing it is our unique *humanity* that draws us together in a "unity" much deeper than what is today, contentiously or disparagingly, called the "gender binary"; and this comes about precisely through the "dispossession" of the cross and the interruption of the Holy Spirit. From here we are escorted into the very inner life of the Trinity, the true locus of our human unity.

It follows that, in Lubich's case, it is less important to place her in a putative typology of "female mysticisms" and much more telling to see her as a spiritual writer who largely transcends such attempts at *differentiating* categorization. Her sole interest, as far as "identity" is concerned, is in the call to the most intimate relation of *all* people, men and women, near and far, friends and enemies, Christians and non-Christians. We could scarcely imagine a more

---

5. See *Essential Writings*, esp. 185–87, and below, 25–29.
6. See John Paul II, *Mulieris dignitatem* (1988, https://www.vatican.va), and *Letter to Women* (1995, https://www.vatican.va).

profound challenge to the anxious and divisive contemporary debates, both personal and political, about "gender" and "identity"; for Lubich's approach implicitly goes underneath and beyond these divisions, inviting all people to experience a depth of cruciform dispossession that is at the same time the complete fulfillment of their human longing for unity and communion. The anxious question about "who am I?"[7] thus finally falls away, since, as Lubich puts it (demandingly, even disturbingly), "We need to know how to lose God within us for God in our brothers and sisters."[8] This is not an erasure of selfhood but its fulfillment, albeit in costly and demanding form.

Renewed Christian Ecumenism or Radical Commitment to the Unity of All Creation?

A second temptation, in relation to reading Chiara Lubich's writings, is to find in her simply the inspiration for a re-energized Christian ecumenical movement. While this is not actually misleading or untrue (the Focolare Movement has indeed from its start been a great instigator of ecumenical understanding), this propulsion alone cannot be said to do justice, once again, to the radicality of Lubich's teaching on "unity." Lubich's own spiritual awakening occurred, of course, in the violent crisis of the last throes of World War II in northern Italy; and it is not a coincidence that the greatest impetus for so many of the emerging Christian ecumeni-

---

7. Famously and poignantly, Dietrich Bonhoeffer asked this question of himself in one of his last poetic meditations before his execution; his final answer was, "Whoever I am, Thou knowest, O God, I am thine!" *Letters and Papers from Prison* (London: Fontana Books, 1959), 173. One might argue that Lubich goes even further in searching for a communitarian selfhood, fused and united in Christ's desolation.

8. Lubich, "Look at All the Flowers," *Essential Writings*, 34.

cal leaders in twentieth-century Europe also came from the shattering impact of the two world wars, resulting finally in the foundation of the World Council of Churches in 1948. Much good, and much productive mutual understanding, has come of such ecumenical work since then (even though the Roman Catholic Church has never formally joined the WCC). But in recent years I think it could be said that many important interdenominational discussions, productive and hopeful up till now, have increasingly bogged down in seemingly irreducible divisions—particularly, again, over matters of sexuality, gender roles, and the question of the ordination of women.[9] What is the way forward?

Once more, Lubich's vision seems to go deeper than this institutional/ecumenical "stuckness," for she invites her followers to go to a profounder level of communion than that which can be achieved by formal ecclesiastical bodies, which—however well orchestrated and well intended—are inevitably dominated by ordained Church leaders committed to defending their particular and distinctive traditions. And this is so because Lubich offers, again, a *more* demanding vision of unity, going well beyond the careful, even nervous, quest for consensus-amid-difference to which the formal ecumenical movement has always (and indeed admirably) been committed. But rather than focusing on the theological minutiae of long-standing ecclesiastical fractures and their potential healing, Lubich demands a recourse, for all, to the primary Johannine vision of unity (Jn 17:21–24), which—on her rendition—can be achieved only by the deepest entering into Christ's own shattered loss of

---

9. I am thinking especially here of the celebrated *ARCIC* Roman Catholic and Anglican discussions (https://iarccum.org/agreed-statements), which, after much initial ecumenical progress and several shared reports, became mired more recently over the question of the ordination of women in the Anglican Communion.

meaning on the cross. The modern theological evocations of this shattering here, of course, are less Johannine as such (John's is, after all, the Gospel in which Jesus dies seemingly without despair and in serene control of his fate) than more strongly reminiscent of von Balthasar's[10] (and on the Protestant side, Moltmann's[11]) accounts of the crisis of the cross and its trinitarian implications. Only the Spirit can bridge the gulf between Father and Son that occurs here—or so this distinctively modern account avers—and with this Lubich's own mystical insights concur: true unity comes at the cost of entering into Christ's very depths of abandonment and human loss, and only moving from there into the regenerative transformation of the Spirit.

"Unity" for Lubich, then, goes well beyond what the prophetic twentieth-century ecumenical movement strove for; for it is also able to embrace and transcend, with new and genuine hope, those points at which that very ecumenical movement has, for now, encountered its own limitations and blockages. (Indeed, we should comment that among the younger generation of church members across denominations, such a sensitivity of empathy and unity appears still to be at work, even despite the caution of official positions. What we might call the "underground" ecumenical work goes on, then, and the Focolare Movement has been very important in this impetus.) Moreover, Lubich's insight here cannot be disconnected from her fundamentally Marian perception of how God works in the world, in and through the discipleship of all those—lay and ordained—who themselves become "Marian" in their way of life, and persistent

---

10. Hans Urs von Balthasar, *Mysterium Paschale: The Mystery of Easter* (San Francisco, CA: Ignatius Press, 2000).

11. Jürgen Moltmann, *The Crucified God: The Cross of Christ as the Foundation and Criticism of Christian Theology* (London: SCM Press, 1974).

and patient in practices of everyday prayer: this is the basic theology of the "hearth." Famously, then, Lubich calls the Focolarini, and any who share their insights and goals, to become "living rosaries,"[12] unified and conjoined to one another through, and alongside, the Mary who herself agreed to be the place of incarnation, and thus the source of ongoing divine transformation. We meet Mary at the "hearth," then, not only as mother but as fellow-traveler and fellow-sufferer in hope.

A New Catholic Theology of the Laity or a More Ambitious Political Revolution from Below?

Finally, I come to the arena in Lubich's thinking and writing that has particularly vibrant importance for the issues in our contemporary world that threaten not only to divide us politically and economically but to undermine the very possibility of our further human flourishing on this planet. Again, it would be tempting to see Lubich's teachings and

---

12. See below, pp. 57–61; and Rowan Williams in *Essential Writings*, xv. Williams is alluding to this reflection by Lubich:
(One day) under a heavy bombardment, after being thrown to the ground and covered with dust that completely filled the air, almost miraculously I was able to stand up . . . and in the midst of the cries of those around me, I felt calm and very much at peace. I realized how deep a sorrow I had just felt in my soul as my life was in danger: it was the sorrow of no longer being able to recite on Earth the Hail Mary.

At that time I did not grasp the sense of those thoughts. Only later, after I had witnessed the beads of living rosary coming together (the first group of Focolarine), and God, selecting people as it were flower by flower, as he composed that Work now entirely Mary's, did I understand the cause of my lament. (*Essential Writings*, 39)

insights merely as an instigation to lay enablement in the Catholic Church (which indeed it is), but perhaps not to the more radical call to a revolution in consciousness that not only includes all people (religious or not, rich or poor) but also a further commitment to the renewal of the earth and its evolutionary fruitfulness. Since this perspective again cuts across tense political divisions, worldwide, it is impossible to read Lubich as an *a*-political thinker; yet, at the same time, because her whole spiritual program is essentially peace-making and encouraging of empathetic attention to the political (or religious) "other," she indicates a practiced way of resisting violence and rhetorical divisiveness at every turn. However, what her work shows us is that we cannot today *presume* the maintenance of modern, civil, Western democracies without working toward undergirding structures of spiritual unity—undergirding groups, like the Focolarini, of those consciously committing themselves to making communities of nurture and peace-making and restitution of the poor and attention to the earth.

In sum, what we learn finally from Chiara Lubich is that while the Marian "hearth" (Focolare) is indeed homely and cozy, the domestic focus around which a loving family may gather, it is also fiery and purgative, a flame spreading and incorporating those who are touched by it into a lifetime of transformation, who then, in turn, touch others. Yes, indeed, in Lubich's vision, lay people, women as much as men, poor as well as rich, are given key roles in the Church, and their ongoing education is a high priority for Lubich; but her vision goes further, too, in its challenging application to contemporary economics, politics, and ecology. Her teaching on poverty, in particular, should make distinctly uncomfortable reading for those who have settled for a mere acceptance of neoliberal capitalism as the world's norm.[13]

Lubich did not live to see many of the alarming new political developments, worldwide, that we confront today, and that eerily remind discerning historians of certain popularist movements of the 1930s, the outcomes of which Lubich lived through in her early years. Her thought, however, presciently anticipates these repetitions, and should not only inspire in us a spiritual response but give real *hope* that such a response is still humanly possible, out of the desolation of Christ's death and into the unifying life of the Spirit. Such a "spirituality" is nothing if not "political," in Lubich's particular sense. In her own words: "Who, then, is more a politician than Mary? [Our task] is to contribute toward fulfilling in human history what Mary announces as already accomplished in herself."[14]

Alexandria, VA
September 14, 2025, the Feast of the Holy Cross

---

13. See below, 140–44, 150–61.
14. See below, 161.

CHIARA LUBICH

Living Witness to a Charism of Unity

Peter Casarella

Pilgrims from Italy and around the world believe that in the Middle Ages the home of Mary and Joseph, which is also the place of the annunciation, was miraculously transferred from Nazareth to its present site in the Marian Shrine of Loreto. In 1939, the nineteen-year-old Chiara Lubich, then known as Silvia, went to this shrine as part of a pilgrimage organized by Catholic Action.[1] Silvia recounts the following experience from that visit:

> I knelt beside the walls blackened by the lamps. Something new and divine surrounded me, almost crushing me. I contemplated the virgin life of the three [Jesus, Mary, and Joseph]. So, Mary will have lived here—I thought—Joseph will have walked across the room from there to there. The Child Jesus in their midst will have known this place for years. The walls will have resounded with his voice. . . .[2]

---

1. https://chiaralubich.org/en/postbiografia/1939-a-loreto/#_ftn1.
2. Maurizio Gentilini, *Chiara Lubich: Prophet of Unity* (Hyde Park, NY: New City Press, 2020), 74.

The origins of the Focolare Movement can be traced back to everyday experiences like the one that Silvia underwent in Loreto. The "new and divine" experience of the Holy Family that echoed within the walls of that tiny home was a revelation of a new way to be Christian and a new form of participation for a lay woman in the Church.

Herein lies the experience of God in everyday life that undergirds Chiara's mature charism of unity. In Loreto a young woman felt close to the child Jesus, close to the hearth that was his original home. Focolare, the movement she later founded, means "hearth." Silvia glimpsed in an initial way that this "work of Mary" had implications. She did not set out to start a movement. She simply remained open to God with eyes and ears of wonder. At Loreto she nonetheless found a "new vocation" in the Church. The echoes of Jesus that resounded in her ears in Loreto pointed to a task and force for unity that she could continue in her own life and that she was able to inspire others to emulate.

Being close to the hearth describes well the everyday setting for the early origins of the movement. God intervened in the everyday of her life so that she could share this charism with others. Chiara Lubich's mystical journey was thus also fortified by a vision that came from above.[3] She felt the love of God so deeply that she called this intense experience of reality "God-love." This "God-love" left a palpable mark on her, and through her on her companions. She received the charism of unity by witnessing to Jesus so very present to her and in the midst of her circle of companions.

Through the pact that she made, first with her mentor and friend, Igino Giordani ("Foco"), but later with others,

---

3. For a detailed unfolding of the experience of Paradise in 1949, see Chiara Lubich, *Paradise: Reflections on Chiara Lubich's Mystical Journey*, ed. Donald W. Mitchell (Hyde Park, NY: New City Press, 2020).

the mutual relationships between a vertical gift and the horizontal sharing of the same were reconfigured once again.[4] In this experience from 1949 of "Paradise," God showered Chiara with the light of God's own triune love for the sake of allowing a new perception of unity to permeate the Church and the world. Chiara was touched by *l'unico Gesù*, "a single Jesus."[5] *This* Jesus is the very opposite of a Jesus who drives us away from others as a form of self-righteousness and that gravitates toward individualism and social alienation. *This* "single Jesus" allows us to see the other *in* ourselves. In sum, that gift and that form of openness to receiving a gift recapitulate the entire spirituality of Chiara Lubich.

Where does this spirituality fit into the Christian and Catholic tradition? The Dominicans talk about *contemplata tradere*, handing over the fruits of contemplation, and the followers of Ignatius of Loyola speak about "seeing God in all things" as a deep plunge that serves as a first step in preparing to be sent into the world on a mission from Christ. But Chiara experienced "God-love" in and from the triune God in such a manner as to communicate the intensity and reality of that experience into a charism of real and palpable unity. On this point, Focolare theologian Jesus Castellano writes: "Chiara Lubich succeeded with a bold intuition in unifying the classical paths of spirituality—the purgative way, the illuminative way, and the unitive way—with the force of love, a love in the form of a

---

4. Jesus Castellano, "Una spiritualità che unisce il vertice del divino e dell'umano," in Chiara Lubich, *La dottrina spirituale* (Rome: Città Nuova Editrice, 2006), 27–33. My translation.

5. Chiara Lubich, *Paradise '49*, para. 1252, summer 1950. "*L'unico*" here points to the singularity of Jesus. See also Fabio Ciardi, "Chiara Lubich, mediatrice di un carisma per l'unità," in Stefan Tobler and Judith M. Povilus, eds., *L'unità: uno sguardo dal Paradiso '49 di Chiara Lubich* (Rome: Città Nuova Editrice, 2021), 127–43.

charity that all at once purifies, illumines, and unifies [us] to God and with God."[6]

This vision is rooted in the radical meditation on unity in the triune God articulated in the Gospel of John: "I in them and you in me, that they may become completely one, so that the world may know that you have sent me and have loved them even as you have loved me" (Jn 17:23). The unity of persons in the triune God leaves a dynamic trace in individuals who remain open to knowing and loving the Son sent by the Father in the Spirit. In this way, the radical difference between divine and human communion is not bridged in any fathomable sense, but the communication of grace and the divine offer of friendship cross the divide.

Chiara was also drawn to Michelangelo's breathtaking *Pietà*. The suffering depicted on the face of the deposed Christ points to a central theme in the spirituality of Chiara Lubich—Jesus Forsaken. The unity that stems from the triune love is shared in the spirit of Jesus's abandonment such that this love encompasses all who suffer under and with Christ's human gaze. Teresa of Avila wrote in her *Interior Castle* about the inner depths of the human soul as a point of departure for an apostolic life and a "mysticism of service."[7] Chiara complements and reinforces this intense vision with an equally thorough meditation on the "exterior castle" of love in which the triune life of God is expressed as an outward gift that takes the form of a communitarian sharing of holiness.

Chiara's spirituality originated in and around Trent. The city had resources for religious formation, and the Capuchins at a local parish lent Franciscan accents to the original impulses she and her companions felt, including

---

6. Castellano, "Una spiritualità," 32. My translation.
7. Castellano, "Una spiritualità," 33.

the chosen name "Chiara." She was baptized "Silvia" but adopted as her own the name of St. Clare of Assisi. These young women in Trent who surrounded her were looking for a new and different way of living out the Gospel at a time when clericalism was a norm and young lay women had no real path for public discipleship in the Church apart from entering a convent.

On May 13, 1944, an Allied bombing raid destroyed much of the city, including her family's home. She, as well as her original companions, young Catholic lay women such as Dori Zamboni and Graziella de Luca, was traumatized by the wreckage that surrounded them.[8] Nevertheless, their fidelity to the Gospel and to Jesus Forsaken compelled them to remain. An intense spiritual commitment summoned Chiara and her cohort to live the unity that the Gospel called them to embody in war-torn Trent. The apostolic life that they shared through the unusual practice of reading the Bible and putting its words into practice became translated into a hitherto-unknown form of life and new mode of engagement with the suffering and woundedness they confronted in their beloved city. Even as Trent was being bombed, Chiara and her companions put themselves at the service of those most in need, despite suspicion that they were collaborating with the Nazis because they loved even their enemies. Misperceptions of the aims of the original cohort abounded. Some called them Communists because they proclaimed an ideal of unity, and some called them Protestants because they were reading Scripture without the guidance of a priest.

Chiara and her companions generated this new way of life through a "pact"—not like signing a legal document but

---

8. See Jim Gallagher, *A Woman's Work: Chiara Lubich* (Hyde Park, NY: New City Press, 1997), 24–30; and Lubich, *Paradise*, 111–26.

a genuine accord. It provided a concrete form for their spirituality, the new collective entity which they called "Soul." They coined the term "trinitizing" to demarcate the new "space" of their encounter with God and one another.[9] This revelation of the Trinity afforded a new way of life. Participating in the pact did not nullify their individual identities. The collective dimension of the spirituality enhances the gift of difference rather than canceling it out. Foco, Dori, Graziella, and the others each maintained a unique calling and a particular form of service.

In Giordani's case, this involved working with Christian Democrats like the future prime minister Alcide de Gasperi in the realm of political theory and action. For Chiara, politics served as "the love of all loves, gathering the resources of people and groups into the unity of a common design so as to provide the means for each one to fulfill in complete freedom his or her specific vocation."[10] Loving a rival political party as one's own is accordingly not only encouraged but necessary. The love of God encompasses all spheres of reality and the good of the community itself. There is a "coincidence of opposites" (Nicholas of Cusa) that unites the infinite Word of God with the finite bearers of that word: "Participating in the divine Life, therefore, does not mean our receiving a part, but our having the whole if it is in us, we who are particulars. . . . The new song is the harmony of harmonies![11] The pact made possible the trinitizing of their

---

9. Piero Coda, "Introduction," in Lubich, *Paradise*, 31.

10. Chiara Lubich, "A United Europe for a United World," address to One Thousand Cities for Europe, a conference for European mayors, Innsbruck, Austria, November 9, 2001, in Chiara Lubich, *Essential Writings: Spirituality, Dialogue, Culture* (Hyde Park, NY: New City Press, 2007), 254–55.

11. Chiara Lubich, as cited in Maria Theresa Henderson, "Gli infiniti toni della voce del Padre," *Nuova Umanità* 25 (2003): 374.

lives and the lives of those whom they encountered. Consequently, they embarked together on a mission to seek unity even in those desperate spaces where, as in war-torn Trent, unity seemed impossible.

All that the young Chiara did, wrote, and thought has a reflective dimension. She possessed an uncanny self-awareness and intelligence that others noticed and admired. In the fall of 1943, she enrolled at Ca' Foscari University in Venice to pursue these ambitions and subsequently gave private lessons but suspended her studies due to the war, having passed up a scholarship in order to remain alongside family and friends who were in dire need. The form of this sharing of wisdom was very much her own. She never pursued "Catholic answers" as isolated fragments but rather sought to abide in the light and love of the triune God in order to allow her responses to arise in the midst of her encounters with diverse interlocutors.

Chiara taught a spirituality of the abandoned Jesus oriented toward the personal and social struggles of daily life. Some questioned her relationship to the doctrine of the Church, but neither she nor the movement she started was ever found deficient. Her spirituality did not intend a watering down of Church doctrine. Her charism, which emerged in the 1940s, offers a new opportunity for renewal within and outside the Church. Although it predates Vatican II by almost thirty years, it follows the pattern of renewal established at the council. It is thus a spirituality that allows a new Pentecost.[12] The Holy Spirit guided Chiara and her earliest companions and reinforced their experience of the Word of God. The Spirit brings them together into the Soul

---

12. Chiara Lubich, *The Holy Spirit: Renewing the Face of the Earth*, ed. Florence Gillet and Raul Silva (Hyde Park, NY: New City Press, 2018), 24–27.

by aligning their hearts to one another and inviting them to experience Christ in the Eucharist:

> The Holy Spirit is the one who makes us one heart, because he links us to one another. He is Love and he makes us one heart. He is the one who, from the beginning, urged us to go to Mass and receive the Eucharist. We weren't the ones who got the idea to receive communion every day. He was the one who told us, because he knew what the Eucharist brings about.[13]

Word and Spirit complement one another, joining together Chiara and her followers to serve as disciples of Jesus Christ.

Chiara's charism of unity was passed on to a new generation, even during her lifetime, for she never conceived that charism to be a possession that she could retain. She was given the gift to teach others to share God's unique gift of love. Saint John Paul II recognized this charism when he endorsed the spirituality of communion in his letter on the new evangelization for the third millennium of Christianity.[14] The Polish pope knew that her charism was a gift to the Church and the world and could be witnessed and promoted in every place and through diverse cultures.

The charism of unity has a special meaning and importance in an age dominated by polarization.[15] The *Instrumentum laboris* for the Second Session of the Synod on Synodality has prophetically identified polarization and the violence it begets as real challenges in the Church today and in con-

---

13. Lubich, *The Holy Spirit*, 26.
14. St. John Paul II, *Novo millennio ineunte*, apostolic letter of January 2001, §43.
15. See Robert Aaron Wessman, *The Church's Mission in a Polarized World* (Hyde Park, NY: New City Press, 2023).

temporary life.[16] The morass of name-calling, dismissal, and instant retribution that surrounds families and communities is unparalleled in recent history. Synodality can provide an antidote to this illness:

> Synodality is implemented through networks of people, communities, bodies and a set of processes that enable an effective exchange of gifts between the Churches and an evangelizing dialogue with the world. Walking together as baptized persons in the diversity of charisms, vocations and ministries, as well as in the exchange of gifts between Churches, is an important sacramental sign for today's world, which, on the one hand, experiences increasingly intense forms of interconnectedness, and on the other is immersed in a mercantile culture that marginalizes gratuitousness.[17]

Synodal networks need time to germinate and grow. Chiara Lubich knew that there can be no "Kumbaya moment" that will make divisions disappear all at once. Instead, Lubich and Pope Francis urge us to enter with the serenity of Jesus Christ directly into this rancor in order to discern a patient path to dispelling misconceptions and false antinomies.

Chiara Lubich's charism of unity beckons us to find a new starting point for addressing polarization. This call converges with main themes of Pope Francis, who at the beginning of his pontificate in 2013 announced the open-

---

16. *Instrumentum laboris* for the Second Session of the Synod on Synodality, §111, available on-line at https://press.vatican.va/content/sala stampa/en/bollettino/pubblico/2024/07/09/240709d.html.

17. *Instrumentum laboris* for the Second Session on the Synod on Synodality, §42.

ing of the cause for Chiara Lubich's canonization. Ten years later, he reconfirmed the role in the Church for her and her charism: "Today, unfortunately, the world is still torn by many conflicts and continues to need artisans of fraternity and peace among individuals and nations."[18] Thus, the spirituality of communion and dialogue that she generated aligns with the model of the polyhedron that the Argentine pope introduced at the beginning of his pontificate in *The Joy of the Gospel*.[19] The sphere, says Pope Francis, homogenizes difference. The polyhedron, on the other hand, preserves difference within the unity created by the Spirit. Chiara Lubich has fostered dialogues of peace and ecumenical, interreligious, and intercultural dialogues that embody Pope Francis's polyhedric model.[20] The way families, communities, regions, and countries are being infected daily with the virus of polarization demonstrates the timeliness of Chiara's artisanship of fraternity and peace.

The spirituality of communion has been lived and can be lived in almost any place; the Focolare now numbers over 140,000 formally professed members and about four million sympathizers in 182 countries around the world. In each place the movement that Chiara initiated draws on the genius of that particular culture. Given the consumerist and individualistic lifestyles that dominate contemporary Western cultures in Europe and North America, the com-

---

18. Pope Francis, "Il Papa ai Focolari: siate artigini di pace in un mondo dilaniato dai conflitti," https://www.vaticannews.va/it/papa/news/2023-12/papa-francesco-focolari-80-anni-chiara-lubich-pace-guerra.html. My translation.

19. Pope Francis, apostolic exhortation *The Joy of the Gospel*, §236.

20. See Peter Casarella, "Wholes and Parts: Ecumenism and Interreligious Encounters in Pope Francis's *Teología del Pueblo*," in *The Whole Is Greater Than Its Parts: Ecumenism and Inter-Religious Encounters in the Age of Pope Francis*, ed. Peter Casarella and Gabriel Said Reynolds (New York: Crossroad, 2020), 31–70.

munitarian elements in this spirituality might seem highly problematic.

Tom Masters and Amy Uelmen have written incisively about "*E pluribus unum*—The Focolare Spirituality and the Quest for Community in a Pluralistic Society."[21] They note that an inculturated spirituality of communion fosters building diverse communities comprised of both religious and civic groups at local levels, thus countermanding effectively the North American tendency "to bowl alone."[22] The charism lived by Focolare members in the United States has also served as a witness to healing the sin of racism. After Chiara Lubich's unprecedented visit to Harlem in 1997, she made a historic and mutually binding pact with Imam W. D. Mohammed and those who have followed his path. Subsequently, the ongoing efforts to foster Muslim-Christian dialogue represent noteworthy healing of social and religious divisions. Finally, the witness of Focolare in the United States to Jewish-Christian dialogue has involved key clerics and bishops, thus offering a model and witness for the whole Church.

In offering a brief glimpse of her life and thought, the editors of this volume are particularly struck by the resonances that can serve as a spirituality for young people as well as the educators, teachers, and pastoral workers who accompany them. Pope Francis rightfully describes the young people today as the "now" of God: "You are the *now* of God, and he wants you to bear fruit. For 'it is in giving that we receive.' The best way to prepare a bright future is to experience the present as best we can, with commit-

---

21. Thomas Masters and Amy Uelmen, *Focolare: Living a Spirituality of Unity in the United States* (Hyde Park, NY: New City Press, 2011), 172–91.

22. Robert D. Putnam, *Bowling Alone: The Collapse and Revival of American Community* (New York: Simon & Schuster, 2000).

ment and generosity."²³ Chiara Lubich's entire itinerary is dedicated to forging a spirituality that speaks to the *"now of God."* She crafted a path that always seeks to discern the signs of the times read in the light of the Gospel, even when these glints of illumination are found at the far edge of what separates the present from the future.²⁴

Guided by her mystical vision, Chiara drew on the past for wisdom but always looked to the future to discover new ways to apply that wisdom to the present and emerging needs of the Church and the world. She teaches us to look at the important task of using a new lens to train as leaders those who are disempowered and at the margins. Like Catherine of Siena and Dorothy Day, she was a creative innovator of Jesus's own start-up.

Of particular interest in this regard is the "Abba School" that Chiara founded, which subsequently aided efforts to establish in 2008 the Sophia University Institute in Loppiano, Italy.²⁵ The Abba School is actually a circle of experts from diverse disciplines who, while Chiara was alive, met regularly with her to concretize the meaning of the spirituality of communion for their work. We have included

---

23. Pope Francis, post-synodal exhortation of March 25, 2019, *Christus vivit*, §187.

24. See *Gaudium et spes*, Pastoral Constitution on the Church in the Modern World, §4. In 2000, I met Chiara in person while serving on a faculty panel during the awarding of her honorary doctorate in education. I asked her to speak about the challenges represented by the internet for young people in the future. At that juncture, worries about screen addiction and the like would have been labeled hyperbolic. She calmly laid out the plans she was developing to introduce Net1, a new collaborative effort to think about digital technology in the light of the Gospel of Jesus Christ. No one today can question the validity of her insights.

25. Chiara Lubich, *An Introduction to the Abba School: Conversations from the Focolare's Interdisciplinary Study Center* (Hyde Park, NY: New City Press, 2002).

excerpts in this volume that speak to the Abba School's accomplishments. At its beginning, the late philosopher and bishop of Aachen, Klaus Hemmerle, played a key role in guiding that work. Today theologian Piero Coda leads it. The Abba School witnesses to the abiding value of "reflection sustained by and centered in a life of community and entailing a transformation of one's being and consciousness through prayer, the suffering of differences, and the like, all of which presuppose the duration of time."[26] As David L. Schindler also notes, the charge that it is unrealistic to expect that such patient work in listening to the wisdom of the Spirit can emerge through sustained dialogue is itself a hastily erected and unnecessary roadblock to future unity.

Thus, in her "reading" of Catholic mystical and intellectual traditions Chiara Lubich opens them up to an ecumenical, interreligious, and global community of interlocutors. The Second World War cut her formal studies short, so her writings were never submitted to peer review. On the other hand, she created paths of thinking and action that will allow those who are curious and willing to explore, for example, the interstices between theology and physics or between spirituality and economics. Chiara Lubich never wrote a monumental work like John Henry Newman's *The Idea of a University*. But the building blocks for returning to this urgent task with fresh new eyes can be found in this volume.

Chiara Lubich's flame of love was not at all extinguished with her passing in 2008. Many concrete examples of her generativity followed.[27] Chiara was generative as the bearer

---

26. David L. Schindler, "Introduction," in Lubich, *An Introduction to the Abba School*, 14.

27. First-person accounts by young people of their experience of the Focolare charism of unity can be found in the introductory chapter, "I Want What You Have," in Thomas Masters and Amy Uelmen, *Focolare:*

of the charism of unity and as the founder of a movement that has focused from an early stage on the living transmission of faith to the next generation. She believed in teaching the faith, but she did not just promote catechesis in isolation from accompaniment. She encouraged the young people in her movement, whom she called "Gen"—the new generation—to form musical performance groups and other creative outlets.[28] In short, she offered them an example of a total form of life, and the youth have responded over and over again with equal joy, commitment, and a desire to generate their own new forms of life-giving unity. Contemporary examples include the creative witness of the charism of unity within the expanding culture of home-schooling families[29] and the vibrant witness of Focolare youth in a group called NextNow, which is dedicated to Catholic-Muslim interreligious cooperation.[30]

There are also young people who followed a path of Christian holiness under the inspiration of Chiara Lubich. The moving witness of a young woman who gave her life to Christ, Blessed Chiara Luce Badano, is an excellent example.[31] Even as she bore the excruciating pain of osteosarcoma

---

Living a Spirituality of Unity in the United States (Hyde Park, NY: New City Press, 2011).

28. These groups, formed in the 1960s, are still active today. Gen Rosso (https://www.genrosso.com/) and Gen Verde (https://www.genverde.it/en/bio/) are the men's and women's performance groups.

29. Experiences of these families are outlined in Michael James, Thomas Masters, and Amy Uelmen, *Education's Highest Aim: Teaching and Learning through a Spirituality of Communion* (Hyde Park, NY: New City Press, 2010), 71–80.

30. See Roberto Catalano, *The Pact: The Spiritual Friendship between Chiara Lubich and Imam W. D. Mohammed* (Hyde Park, NY: New City Press, 2024), 61–70.

31. Her story is recounted in a collection assembled by the Chiara Badano Foundation, *"In My Staying Is Your Going": The Life and Thoughts of Chiara Luce Badano* (Hyde Park, NY: New City Press, 2021), and in

(bone cancer), she received the strength to bring other young people to the Jesus who, she assured them, was in their midst. As she would say, "If you want it, Jesus, I want it too."[32]

This volume does not seek to enumerate the many activities, gatherings, and programs that Chiara Lubich has generated among young people. But it is important to note the generativity of the charism and how it responds to the very eager desire of youth to overcome divisions of the past and to heal the many gaping wounds that afflict our society and our planet.

The movement of the Spirit that Chiara Lubich started while surveying the rubble of her beloved Trent in World War II is hardly finished. Its reverberating presence is felt throughout the globe among believers and nonbelievers.[33] The work of Mary that she initiated almost a century ago has just begun.

This volume offers only a taste of Chiara Lubich's spirituality of unity.[34] It aims to cover the most essential ele-

---

Geraldine Guadagno and Loretta Rauschuber, *Blessed Chiara Badano: Her Secrets to Happiness* (Hyde Park, NY: New City Press, 2021).

32. *In My Staying Is Your Going*, 48.

33. The Focolare Movement's most current statistics, from 2022, indicate the following:
- Interreligious dialogue: 100,000 members engaged, with 20 religious leaders involved at a world-wide level, reaching 6 million people in collaboration with partners of various religions.
- Ecumenical dialogue: 8,000 members engaged, with 600 Christian leaders, 300 communities and movements connected through "Together for Europe."
- Dialogue with those not affiliated with any particular faith tradition: 14 groups with 400 collaborators.
- Dialogue with contemporary culture: 72 professional groups; including 1,850 professionals and academics.

See BdC-2022-DialogoIT at www.focolare.org.

34. See, for example, Chiara Lubich, *Essential Writings* (Hyde Park, NY: New City Press, 2007).

ments by focusing on short but illuminating excerpts from her own many writings and speeches. The bibliography at the end provides additional resources for those who would like to delve deeper into Chiara's life and thought.

The chapter headings are accordingly divided as follows:
1. Origins and Trajectories
2. Going to God Together
3. Spirituality of Communion: Living Jesus Within
4. Spirituality of Communion: Living Jesus in Relationships

The first chapter establishes the historical setting from which the spirituality of communion emerges, as well as the cradle in which it was born—the pact that brought Chiara and her companions to understand the dimensions of the unity that they had begun to live in Trent. The second chapter looks at the trinitarian foundations of her thinking as well as the concrete realization of this form of life in Mary Desolate, Jesus Forsaken, and the Eucharist. The third and fourth chapters offer details regarding the spiritual and theological contours of the life lived by Chiara's followers. Chapter 3 looks at Jesus's presence amid personal struggles. Chapter 4 moves to the same theme seen through the exterior castle, the life of communion lived in and through relationships.

The excerpts in this volume come from a variety of published writings, especially from the authoritative English-language collection of her principal texts, *Essential Writings*. Some unpublished material from the Paradise '49 experience as well as from a Focolare database of unpublished documents was provided by the Focolare Archive (*Archivio Generale Movimiento Focolari* [AGMF]). All these citations are acknowledged at the end of each excerpt with reference to the bibliography at the end of the book.

Living Witness to a Charism of Unity | xxxiii

The editors are grateful to Robert Ellsberg and his team for allowing the charism of Chiara Lubich to find its place in this series. Chiara would surely be pleased to be in communion with the many women and men who are represented in it and who have served as spiritual masters in diverse ways. Furthermore, by sharing her own life and witness she would welcome the opportunity to engage a new generation of seekers of spiritual wisdom.

Timeline of Significant Events

January 22, 1920
Chiara Lubich is born in Trent, Italy, and baptized "Silvia." Her mother is a practicing Catholic; her father, a printer by trade, is a socialist. Her brother, Gino, will become an anti-Fascist resistance fighter, and later write for *L'Unità*, the official newspaper of the Italian Communist Party.

1938
Qualified as a primary school teacher, she begins her career at Castello and at Livio, small villages in the Val di Sole near Trent. Later, she will teach in Trent itself. She begins studies in philosophy at the University of Venice, but the Second World War will prevent her from completing them.

1939
During a program for young people of Catholic Action she visits the Marian shrine at Loreto, where she discovers her vocation. It would be the "focolare," a community of both virgins and married people who give their lives completely to God.

1943
As a member of the Franciscan Third Order, attracted by the radical choice of God by Clare (in Italian, "Chiara") of Assisi, she takes the name "Chiara" as her own.

December 7, 1943
She gives herself to God with a perpetual vow of chastity. This date has come to be considered the birth of the Focolare Movement.

May 13, 1944
The aerial bombardment of Trent. Chiara Lubich's house is damaged, and her family has to flee. She decides to remain in the city so as to sustain the small group growing up around her. After a short time, they are offered an apartment in Piazza Cappucini, which, recalling her experience at Loreto, she calls the "little house of Nazareth." She and her first companions take up residence there, becoming in fact the first "focolare."

1947
The Movement receives its first diocesan approval. Carlo de Ferrari, archbishop of Trent, recognizes that "Here, there is the hand of God."

1948
The first men's focolare opens, in Trent. In Rome, in the Italian Parliament building, she meets the Honorable Igino Giordani, a father of four, an elected representative, writer, journalist, and ecumenical pioneer. He later will become the first married focolarino. She sees him as a cofounder of the Movement because of his contribution to the spirituality of unity's incarnation in society and to its developments in the field of ecumenism.

1949–1959
Beginning in the summer of 1949, each year Chiara and her first companions go to the mountains near Trent.

On July 16, 1949, together with Igino Giordani and her first companions, Chiara enters into a period of profound spiritual insight, which comes to be known as "Paradise '49."[1]

In subsequent years, more and more persons join them in the mountains. They find themselves becoming the temporary presence of a new society based on the Gospel: the *Mariapolis* (the city of Mary). In 1959, more than ten thousand people from twenty-seven nations, and from as far away as Taiwan and Brazil, gather at Fiera di Primiero, near Trent.

1953

She founds the branch of the married focolarini, who are consecrated to God according to their state in life. Later, they become part of the women's and men's focolares. In time, they come to lead the *New Families* Movement.

1954

She founds the branch of the diocesan priests and of members of religious orders who take part in the Movement. Pasquale Foresi, the first priest focolarino, is ordained by the archbishop of Trent. Chiara Lubich also sees him as a cofounder because of his role in developing the Movement: for instance, in furthering theological studies, in drawing up the statutes, in setting up the first publishing house, and in establishing Loppiano, the first of the Movement's little towns.

1956

The mimeographed first edition of *Città Nuova* (New City), the Movement's magazine, is issued. Chiara promotes the

---

1. See Chiara Lubich, *Paradise: Reflections on Chiara Lubich's Mystical Journey*, ed. Donald W. Mitchell (Hyde Park, NY: New City Press, 2020).

volunteers of God, lay men and women of the Movement committed to bringing God, the source of freedom and unity, into every corner of society.

1959
The first collection of her spiritual writings, *Meditations*, is published, marking the start of the *Città Nuova* publishing house. This effort continues today with sixteen distinct publishing houses around the world, including *Ciudad Nueva* in Latin America, Focolare Media in North America, etc.

1960
As the result of a meeting in 1954 with refugees from what was then Czechoslovakia, she begins spreading the Focolare in the countries of Eastern Europe under Communist rule.

1961
In Darmstadt, Germany, she meets some Lutheran pastors who wish to learn about her Gospel-based spirituality: the start of the Movement's ecumenical activities.

1962
The Movement receives its first papal approval. Pope John XXIII recognizes it with the name *The Work of Mary*.

1964
At Rocca di Papa, near Rome, Chiara Lubich inaugurates the first *Mariapolis Center* for the formation of the Movement's members; at Incisa Valdarno, near Florence, she establishes Loppiano, the first of the Movement's little towns that give witness to the life of the Gospel.

1966

In London, she is received by Dr. Michael Ramsey, archbishop of Canterbury and primate of the Anglican Communion. He encourages the spreading of the Focolare spirituality within the Church of England. Subsequently, she will meet his successors: Drs. Donald Coggan, Robert Runcie, George Carey, and Rowan Williams.

She establishes the *Gen*, the branch of the Movement for young adults. In Fontem, Cameroon, she lays the cornerstone for a hospital dedicated to lowering the high rate of infant mortality among the Bangwa tribe. A little town is begun. It gives witness to the unity and the working together of the Focolare Movement and the Bangwa people. In 2000, she launches a widespread project to spread Gospel-based values to neighboring peoples as well.

1967

In Istanbul, she meets with the ecumenical patriarch of the Orthodox Church, His All Holiness Athenagoras I. Between 1967 and 1972 she travels to Istanbul eight times and is received on twenty-three occasions by the patriarch. Subsequently, she will meet with his successors, Demetrios I and Bartholomew I.

She founds the *New Families* Movement.

1968

She founds the *Gens*, a branch for seminarians.

1970

She founds a movement for children and younger teenagers, ages nine to seventeen—the *Gen 3*, the third generation of the Movement.

1971
At a historic meeting with Chiara, Pope Paul VI gives his blessing to the *Women Religious, Adherents to the Focolare Movement*.

1975
During the Holy Year, she presents to Pope Paul VI twenty thousand young people from five continents, gathered for the *Genfest*, an international youth festival repeated every five years.

1976
There begins a series of international meetings for *Bishops Friends of the Focolare Movement*, promoted by Klaus Hemmerle, bishop of Aachen, Germany. These events allow the bishops to deepen the spirituality of unity and to have a lived experience of "effective and affective" collegiality. Chiara Lubich considers Bishop Hemmerle a cofounder of the Movement for his doctrinal contributions as well as for bringing to life the branch of the bishops that has spiritual ties with the Movement. It will receive papal approval in 1998.

1977
In London, before representatives of many faith traditions, she receives the Templeton Prize for Progress in Religion. Dialogue with world religions gets underway.

1981
In Tokyo, Rev. Nikkyo Niwano, founder of a lay Buddhist renewal movement, the Rissho Kosei-Kai, invites her to speak in its great temple before ten thousand people. A dialogue begins that continues to develop through efforts to provide humanitarian relief and to promote peace.

1982
At the request of Pope John Paul II, *Bishops Friends of the Focolare* from various Churches hold their first annual meeting.

1984
She founds the movement for younger children aged four to eight, the *Gen 4*. Pope John Paul II visits the International Center of the Movement in Rocca di Papa, near Rome.

1985
She is named consultant to the Pontifical Council for the Laity. She participates in the extraordinary synod held on the twentieth anniversary of the Second Vatican Council. Subsequently, she will be invited to the 1987 Synod on the Vocation and Mission of the Laity, as well as to the 1990 Synod for Europe.

1990
The Pontifical Council for the Laity approves the updated *General Statutes of the Work of Mary*, also known as *The Focolare Movement*. Working together with Bishop Klaus Hemmerle, she establishes at the Center of the Movement the *Abba School* to explore the ramifications of the charism of unity for diverse disciplines, including theology, philosophy, social sciences, and natural sciences.

1991
In *Mariapolis Ginetta*, near São Paolo, Brazil, responding to the deep division between the rich and the poor, she establishes the *Economy of Communion*, which soon spreads throughout the world.

1994
She is named one of the honorary presidents of the World Conference on Religion and Peace (WCRP).

1996

In Naples, Italy, with a group of politicians, she forms the *Movement for Unity in Politics*. She proposes that they, although having differing political affiliations, base their lives and their political duties on fraternity.

From the University of Lublin, Poland, she receives an honorary doctoral degree in Social Sciences for the innovative influence of the spirituality of unity. Subsequently, she will receive thirteen other honorary doctoral degrees: Theology (in the Philippines and in Taiwan, 1997; Slovakia, 2003), Social Communications (Thailand, 1997), Humane Letters (Sacred Heart University, Fairfield, Connecticut, 1997), Philosophy (Mexico, 1997), a joint degree from all thirteen Academic Faculties (Argentina, 1998), Humanities and the Science of Religion (Brazil, 1998), Economics (Brazil, 1998; Italy 1999), Psychology (Malta, 1999), Education (Catholic University of America, Washington, DC, 2000), Theology of Consecrated Life (Rome, 2004).

In Paris, she receives the UNESCO Prize for Peace Education.

1997

In Bangkok, Thailand, she meets with the supreme Buddhist patriarch of Thailand, His Holiness Somdet Phra Nyanasamvara, who encourages dialogue and cooperation between Buddhists and the Focolare Movement.

At Chiang Mai, Thailand, she presents her spiritual experience to a sizable number of monks, nuns, and lay Buddhists.

In Manila, she speaks of the Focolare Movement to the general assembly of the Philippine Bishops' Conference. Following this, she will make presentations to the Bishops' Conferences of Taiwan, Switzerland, Argentina, Brazil,

Croatia, Slovenia, Poland, India, the Czech Republic, Slovakia, Austria, India, and Ireland.

In New York, at the Glass Palace of the United Nations, she speaks on the unity of peoples to a symposium organized by the WCRP.

Invited by its founder, Imam W. D. Mohammed, she speaks before three thousand African American members of the American Muslim Society at the Malcolm X Mosque in Harlem, New York. Afterwards, they seal a "pact, in the name of the one God, to work unceasingly for peace and for unity."[2]

The first International Ecumenical Congress meets at Castel Gandolfo, Italy. Set up by the Focolare Movement, it gathers 1,200 participants representing seventy churches and fifty-six nations.

At Graz, Austria, she sets forth the spirituality of unity as "an ecumenical spirituality" at the opening of the Second European Ecumenical Assembly, sponsored by the Council of European Bishops' Conferences and by the Conference of European Churches, including the Orthodox, Anglican, and Protestant Churches. In 2002 she also presents this concept to the World Council of Churches in Geneva, Switzerland.

1998

At Castel Gandolfo, Italy, she addresses a conference on "Dialogue with People of Various Convictions." It attracts nearly two hundred participants, many with no particular religious affiliation, who have been drawn for some time by the spirit of the Movement, particularly by the universal values it promotes. She proposes that they work together to bring about universal brotherhood.

---

2. See Roberto Catalano, *The Pact: The Spiritual Friendship between Chiara Lubich and Imam W. D. Mohammed* (Hyde Park, NY: New City Press, 2024).

At Buenos Aires, Argentina, she meets with the Jewish community.

The president of Brazil confers on her the "Cruziero do Sul" (Southern Cross) for her efforts on behalf of the most disadvantaged and for promoting the Economy of Communion.

In Rome, at St. Peter's Square, before more than 350,000 participants, she is one of four founders who speak at the first international meeting of Ecclesial Movements and New Communities. Pope John Paul II entrusts to her the development of a path to communion among the Movements. Subsequently, among Churches at the local and national level, there will be large-scale meetings which by 2006 reached 282, involving more than 325 Movements and more than a half-million people.

In Strasbourg, France, she receives the 1998 Human Rights Prize from the Council of Europe.

1999

In Strasbourg, France, she speaks to the Conference for the fiftieth anniversary of the Council of Europe. In her address, "A Market-based Society, Democracy, and Solidarity," she presents the experience of the Economy of Communion as the basis of a new way of conducting business.

In Speyer, Germany, she brings a message of encouragement from Pope John Paul II to a meeting of the founders and leaders of forty-one Ecclesial Movements and New Communities, organized by the Community of Sant'Egidio and the Renewal in the Holy Spirit.

2000

In Rothenburg, Germany, she meets with representatives of fifty Evangelical Lutheran Movements.

In Washington, DC, alongside Imam W. D. Mohammed, she speaks to a gathering of more than five thousand people, including Christians and members of the American Muslim Society. A fraternal dialogue begins in many different cities across the United States, a development of particular significance considering the tensions in the United States following September 11, 2001. There are forty mosques in open dialogue with the Movement.

In Rome, at the Italian parliament's Palazzo San Macuto, she presents to a large crowd of politicians the ideals of the *Movement for Unity in Politics*. In Assisi, she advocates a journey toward communion among old and new charisms, beginning with the different branches of the Franciscan family. In Montserrat, Spain, she does the same with the Benedictine family.

2001
In Coimbatore, Tamil Nadu, India, she receives the Defender of Peace Prize from two Gandhian organizations, the Shanti Ashram and the Sarvodaya Movement. She also shares the story of her spiritual journey at the Somaiya University, Mumbai. These events mark the beginning of deep dialogue with Hindus.

In Prague, Czech Republic, she meets with President Vaclav Havel.

In Zurich, Switzerland, she speaks of the spirituality of unity at the Grossmünster, the ancient birthplace of the German-speaking Swiss Reformed Church. In 2002, she also speaks in Geneva at the Cathedral of St. Peter, birthplace of the Reformation as it developed under the influence of William Farel and John Calvin.

At Innsbruck, Austria, she participates at the Convention "1000 Cities for Europe." It is also attended by the then-president of the European Commission, Romano Prodi, by the president of Austria, Thomas Klestil, and by more than seven hundred mayors and local administrators from thirty-five countries in both Eastern and Western Europe. She is invited to speak on fraternity as a political concept.

2002
At the Day of Prayer for Peace in the World, held in Assisi, together with Andrea Riccardi, founder of the Community of Sant'Egidio, she speaks as a representative of the Roman Catholic Church. This event, arranged by Pope John Paul II, includes leaders of the twelve principal world religions.

In Castel Gandolfo, Italy, she supports the first symposium on interreligious dialogue among members of the Abba School and authoritative scholars and professors of Hinduism. There will follow another symposium with Hindus (2004) and symposiums with representatives of Buddhism (2004 and 2006), Judaism (2005), and Islam (2005).

2003
In Mumbai, she deepens the dialogue with Hinduism that began during her first visit to India in 2001. She speaks at the Somaiya College, an Indian institute of higher learning dedicated principally to interreligious dialogue; at the Bharatiya Vidya Bhavan, a center founded to rediscover the cultural roots of Hinduism; and with the Swadhyaya Family, a Movement of more than eight million adherents spread throughout India.

Invited by Cardinal Dias, in Mumbai she also presents the spirituality of unity to priests, members of religious congregations, and lay movements. At the request of Archbishop Conceçao, she repeats the presentation in Delhi.

Responding to Pope John Paul II's request that the Focolare Movement take responsibility for promoting the year dedicated to the Rosary for the peace of the world, she promotes an International Marian Congress at Castel Gandolfo. Based on that event, 157 other Congresses, local as well as national, will follow on all five continents, at both local and national levels.

2006
She is asked by the Pontifical Council for the Laity to speak on behalf of all the Ecclesial Movements and New Communities during their meeting with Pope Benedict XVI in St. Peter's Square on the vigil of Pentecost.

2007
On December 7, Sophia University Institute, born as a further development of the Abba School, is erected by pontifical decree in the Focolare town of Loppiano. This is the last official act signed by Chiara Lubich.

March 14, 2008
Following a long illness, after having been visited in the hospital by the ecumenical patriarch of Constantinople, Bartholomew I, and receiving a comforting personal letter from Benedict XVI, after having been visited at her bedside by hundreds of people, Chiara dies at her home in Rocca di Papa, Italy.

January 28, 2015
Bishop Raffaello Martinelli, of the Diocese of Frascati, Italy, opens the cause of beatification and canonization of Chiara Silvia Lubich, declaring her a Servant of God.

—See Lubich, *Essential Writings*, 383–93

1

ORIGINS AND TRAJECTORIES

Introduction

The beginnings of Chiara Lubich's charism of unity are found in her early life in Trent, when she was nurtured in faith and charity and discerned an initial vocation to be a teacher. This section offers a glimpse of her life from her birth in 1920, through the early years during World War II, to the beginnings of friendships and mystical experiences that would ultimately galvanize a movement within the Church. The experiences of "Paradise" in 1949 are particularly moving and show the deeply inward and at the same time very "outward" appropriation of the love of the triune God that formed her entire spirituality and shaped her vocation as a disciple of Christ and a lay leader in the Church.

This selection, which recounts the first phase of Chiara's life, her education, and her vocation, is taken from Armando Torno's biography. Subsequent selections are taken from her own interviews, letters, and diaries.

Chiara Lubich: Family and Childhood

Chiara Lubich, the second of Luigi and Luigia Lubich's four children, was born in Trent on January 22, 1920. She was baptized "Sylvia" at Saint Mary Major, the church where the third session of the Council of Trent had been held.

The parents often fasted in order to be able to feed their hungry children. Although they were poor, Chiara would later recall, the family always held on to its dignity.

For Luigia, faith was their greatest wealth, and she transmitted this faith to her children. Chiara considered it a most precious gift, affirming that she was always drawn to the "things of God." As a small child, Sylvia attended public elementary school on Via Verde, but since her mother was anxious for her to receive a Catholic formation, she entrusted her daughter to the Sisters of the Child Mary. Sr. Carolina, who was giving religious instruction to a small group of girls, brought them to church every Friday for an hour of adoration before the monstrance. Little Sylvia would fix her gaze on the Eucharist, where it was set among the golden rays of the monstrance, and say: "You have created the sun to give us light and warmth, make your light and your warmth come into my soul through my eyes." Over and over again she would repeat these words until it appeared that the Host had turned black and everything around it had become white. She would stare so intensely that she once fainted because of her concentration and the intensity of her gaze.

Lubich's First Sense of Being Called

Silvia was thirteen years old when, strolling down one of the streets of Trent, coming to the end of Via della Torre, she felt called to be a martyr. She immediately said yes to this calling, which seemed to come from above. A couple of years later, on the feast day of St. Thomas Aquinas, while she was with her classmate Valentina Ghesla, she felt another strong inspiration: holiness. Immediately, she told Valentina: "I want to become a saint." Valentina responded: "Me too." They ran to the Catholic Action center to share this experience with the chaplain, Msgr. Cesconi. Then they were invited to attend gatherings of the group. Chiara first enrolled in the Catholic Youth and later in the student section of the Catholic Action group

Lubich's Education and Career as a Teacher

As a teenager [Sylvia] . . . attended teacher training school at the Rosmini Institute, which exists today. The philosophy instructor—a Tuscan, an atheist who was an eloquent speaker—enchanted the students with his fascinating lectures. Despite her natural shyness, Sylvia did not keep silent when he said things that seemed erroneous to her. She was saddened and disappointed, especially because of the strong influence he had on her classmates. Sylvia frequently interrupted his lectures, exclaiming, "Professor, you're mistaken! It's not like that! It's not true!" Her friend Valentina tried to reason with her. "Sylvia, be careful! If the professor gives you a low mark, your average will drop. This could mean losing your scholarship for the next school year." Nevertheless, Sylvia insisted, "Professor, that's not true!" She did not know how to argue it out; she only felt that he was not telling the truth, and she could not remain silent about it. She was timid and polite, her face would blush as she raised her hand, but she could not keep silent: "It's not true, sir!" The professor would tell her to calm down as he signaled her to take her seat.

At the end of the quarter, her report card arrived with an "A" in Philosophy, the only "A" in the class. For Sylvia this confirmed the value of truth and the need to defend it at any cost. During the second quarter Valentina joined in with Sylvia. "It's not true!" they would exclaim in chorus, as they waved their hands in the air.

They were constantly interrupting, until one day the professor asked them to keep silent for the time being, suggesting a private conversation outside of class. On the other side of the classroom door, Valentina and her classmates—who had been praying for the conversion of their professor—waited for Sylvia to come out. She had already begun her conversation with the professor. They spoke about St. Augustine and who knows what else. Finally, the professor gave in. "Listen, Sylvia, don't say this to anyone. You're correct; but I beg you, don't say it to anyone." Chiara left the classroom in silence and to the inquiries of her classmates responded by saying only, "Let's go to a church and thank God." And so they did.

Much later, Sylvia met this professor on the street. "Sylvia," he told her, "there are many troubles in my family. And so I went to that church where you always go and I prayed to that God whom you love, and I hope he will help me." They never met again. During the war the professor became a captain in the navy and was killed in action.

In 1938, at the age of eighteen, Sylvia received a teaching certificate, with the highest grades. She now dreamed of enrolling at the Catholic University of Milan, where she could hear people talk about God and Truth. Her heart was filled with a singular and consuming desire: to know God. But she came at the top of the list of those who did not win entrance to the scholarship lottery. It was a hard blow, but precisely in the midst of this deep pain she had a spiritual experience that marked her for life. As she sat beside her mother on the divan of their living room, shedding desperate tears because of her great disappointment, she heard a voice say to her, "I myself will be your teacher." Though not fully grasping the significance of these words, she accepted them, and peace returned to her soul.

In those years, Sylvia's spiritual life had no particular focus. She herself had often said that she was simply a Christian, living the Gospel as the Church taught it to her, trying to live it the best she could on her own. She learned it from her mother, from the Sisters of the Child Mary, from her brother, Gino, as well as through her involvement in the Catholic Action group.

Once she received her teaching certificate, she immediately began working at Castello di Ossana, a small town in the Val di Sole region, about forty-five miles northeast of Trent, where she was assigned to teach the elementary grades.

—Armando Torno, *Chiara Lubich*, 16–21

Intuitions at the House of Loreto

I must tell you about the intuition I had in 1939. I was at Loreto for a Catholic Action rally. The first time I went into the Holy House of Loreto I had no time to consider whether this was really the place where historically the Holy Family had lived. I knelt on the floor near the wall blackened by the smoke of the lamps. I couldn't utter a single word; I was seized by the mystery of what had happened in that place. All kinds of ideas about the Holy Family came to me. I said to myself, the child Jesus walked from there to there. The voice of Jesus echoed between these walls, and Mary must have sung here to rock her little child to sleep. Maybe it was Joseph who fixed the beams in place. There was also a window; it came to me that maybe Mary was there at the moment of the Annunciation and that the Angel came in at that window. All these thoughts pressed down on me, heavier and heavier. It was as if someone had placed the dome of St. Peter's on top of me, and I wept until I could weep no more.

That was the intuition that came to you in 1939. But now, after all these years, how do you see the family of Nazareth?

I can picture them to myself because I live in the focolare, which reproduces in some way the presence of Jesus among men. When Jesus is there, we feel an extraordinary peace, a light illuminates us from within, we feel on top form, ready to venture anything, afraid of nothing. Thus if you can think that at Nazareth Jesus was physically present with Mary who was who she was, and with Joseph, who was also someone special, you can imagine what an extraordinary family the Trinity had thought up for the incarnation of the Word!

Was that episode at Loreto the beginning of the revelation of your particular vocation?

No, no! Definitely not. I was completely passive in the face of what was happening to me. It was simply that the Holy House at Loreto so attracted me that every time I could escape from my companions I rushed there, and the same phenomenon was repeated. I think I stayed at Loreto a week or maybe longer. On the last day, when I was at the back of the basilica, which is built over the house, the nave was full of young girls celebrating the conclusion of the rally (wearing white veils, I remember), and an idea crossed my mind: an army of virgins will follow you.

And then I returned home. I met my confessor, who, seeing me quite content and at peace, asked,

"Have you found your way?"
"Yes."
"Are you getting married?"
"No."
"Are you going to lead a consecrated life in the world?"
"No."
"Then are you entering a convent?"
"No, there is a fourth way."

Of course, I knew nothing about this "fourth way," and that is the only moment when I had the intuition that others would follow me.

—Michel Pochet, *Stars and Tears*, 35–37

The Beginnings

The Movement began in Trent. At the outset I had no plan in mind, no program. The idea for this Movement was God's; it was a project from heaven. That is how it was in the beginning; that is how it has been during the fifty-four years of its growth.

In 1943 war raged in Trent: ruin, destruction, death.

For a variety of reasons, a group of young people about my age gathered around me.

One day I found myself with my new companions in a dark, candle-lit cellar, a book of the gospels in hand. I opened it. There was Jesus's prayer before he died: "Father . . . may they all be one" (Jn 17:11, 21). It was not an easy text to start with, but one by one those words seemed to come to life, giving us the conviction that we were born for that page of the gospel. On the feast of Christ the King, we gathered around an altar. We said to Jesus: "You know the way to achieve unity. Here we are. If you so desire, use us." The liturgy of the day amazed us: "Ask of me," it said, "and I will make the nations your heritage, and the ends of the earth your possession" (Ps 2:8).

We asked. God is all-powerful.

The bombardment continued, destroying some of the people and things we cherished. One loved her home; it was ruined. Another was planning to be married; her fiancé did not return from the front. My ideal was to study, but the war kept me from attending the university.

Every event touched us profoundly. The lesson God was giving us in those circumstances was clear: all is vanity of vanities. Everything passes away. At the same time, God put a question into my heart meant for all of us, and with it came an answer: is there an ideal that does not die, that no bomb can destroy, to which we can devote our lives?

Yes, there is. That ideal is God.

We decided to make God the ideal of our lives. In the midst of war, the fruit of hate, God was manifesting himself to us as Love. Our parents sought refuge in the mountain valleys. We stayed in Trent. Some for work or study. I in order to be with the Movement that was coming to life. An apartment with a few rooms became our shelter. We found the ideal to live for. It was God, God-Love.

—Lubich, *Essential Writings*, 4

The First Focolare House

On May 13, 1944, at around one o'clock in the afternoon, the air-raid alarms began to sound, and everyone ran for the shelters. After a few moments of silence, the air attack began. The bombings extended from the area where the Capuchins lived all the way to Via Gocciadoro and beyond; it was a direct hit on the center of the city. The area where Chiara's house was located had also been seriously damaged in the attack. The house was uninhabitable, and that evening Luigi

Lubich decided to move his family to the Parco di Gocciadoro, where they could rest for the night before heading for the mountains to the west of Trent, toward Passo della Fricca, where many had already fled.

That was a terrible night for Chiara; she often referred to it as a night of "stars and tears." It was still cold, and the night sky was clear. Lying on the grass, she stayed awake watching the stars move across the firmament, and she wept at the thought of not being able to accompany her parents into the mountains. She could never abandon her companions in the city. Over and over the words of Virgil's Eclogue X came to her mind: *Omnia vincit amor*, "Love conquers all." But could the love of God also conquer this? Could it let her parents leave without her, when she was their only source of income?

But the will of God seemed too obvious. She couldn't leave Trent; she couldn't leave her companions. At dawn she asked for and received her father's blessing (who surprisingly assented to her request without batting an eye). And after she loaded the heavy backpack onto her mother's shoulders, she watched as her family took the path into the mountains. Turning the other way, she followed the road back into the city, which had been destroyed by the air raid.

On one of the main thoroughfares in the historic district of Trent, Corso 3 Novembre 1918, a desperate and disheveled woman ran up to her. Taking Chiara by the shoulders she screamed, "Four of mine have died! Four!" Chiara consoled her as best she could, firmly deciding that from this moment on, she would put the sorrows and pains of humanity around her in place of the pain she was feeling for having to leave her family. Amid houses and streets reduced to rubble, she went in search of her companions, and found all of them alive.

She also found her brother, Gino, alive at the hospital. He showed her a tangle of bodies and rubble, a group of prostitutes, their faces covered with makeup, dead beneath a fallen wall. The nun who had been taking care of them, however, managed to come out of it alive. "See?" Gino remarked, "Everything is vanity of vanities."

A Franciscan tertiary named Carmela offered Chiara a place to stay at her home by putting another bed in her room. A short time later, Chiara received hospitality from the Sisters of our Lady of Sion. Later still, in the autumn of 1944, they found an old apartment on Piazza Cappuccini, which had been left abandoned by an Italian official who was on the battlefront. This apartment came to be called "the little house." Giosi moved in, while the other companions stayed with their families. But they went to the little house as often as they could.

—Torno, *Chiara Lubich*, 30

Paradise '49: Chiara Lubich's Collective Mystical Experience

Chiara Lubich sums up what she and her companions experienced after living a collective spirituality of unity from 1943, during the terror of the war, to 1949.

The impression of our soul was the impression of rising, rising, rising, rising as if along a ray—we used to say it this way—of the will of God. But to speak in this way diminishes it. It was a getting ever closer to the sun, ever closer to God. What does this "rising" mean? It means that the farther up you go, the more you leave below the things beneath. They are lost. In fact, my new life, the new life that I had in me, the God who lived in me, had in itself the God of yesterday and of the previous day, and the God of a year ago. So, whatever was behind me collapsed into nothing, because it was all *in* me. So, the impression we had was the impression of climbing, so to speak, of rising ever closer to God.

Vacation in the Mountains

That's when 1949 happened. It seems that I had worn myself out a little and was a bit tired. So, the doctor suggested that I take a break in the mountains and leave behind the life of the Movement. And my companions said that I shouldn't go alone and that they would come with me too. So, I agreed of course. But I had no idea what would happen up there. So, having left the Movement behind, we went up into the mountains. I remember . . . the impression that a poster for a film made on us: "Amidst the peaks I'll bear you away." But this was just one sign among many, because God uses many means.

So, when we arrived up in the mountains, I noticed a second phenomenon: that this kind of fire that was inside me—because the Word had become fire as well as Word—was also a voice and that, as soon as it entered into us, the gospel flamed up and I found myself saying: "I have just finished a first phase of living the Word of God; later I will live it again in a different way, because here everything is becoming fire, everything is becoming God." So if, inside me—and inside the *pope*,[1] I think—things were like this; outside us there was something else. The Lord, through an extraordinary grace, showed me all of nature differently from how I see it now, or how you see it now, or how I myself had seen it previously.

---

1. This is a word in the Trentino dialect, loosely translated as "children" or "young girls."

A Spiritual Sun

So, the vision of God beneath all things was very strong—obviously a special grace of God. So, if the pine trees were gilded by the sun, if the streams ran down in their waterfalls glistening in the sunlight, and so on, if the daisies, the other flowers, the sky . . . beneath every created thing that I saw there was a spiritual sun—not the sun—but stronger, and I saw it.

You might ask me: "What did you see, Chiara?"

With the soul.

"But what did you see?"

God who sustains all things. God who holds everything up.

"But how did you see it?"

So, I saw that God beneath things made them be not as we see them; they were all linked among themselves by love, all in love with one another.

So if the stream flowed into the sea, it was out of love. If one pine tree rose up beside another, it was out of love. Saying "out of love" is unclear. I saw love, which is God, beneath things, which bound all things together. And this was a blinding sun. And so, the vision of this unity that God gave us or, even better, the vision of God who united everything in creation, was stronger than the things themselves.

I was at this point in the spiritual life when, at a certain moment, Foco came to the mountains. Until that point, I had felt the need to meet someone who . . . , because I felt that the Ideal wasn't a common thing. The *pope* who were with me, in contrast, believed that everything was normal.

I had a sense that there was something different from Christianity as normally understood. Deep down inside, I felt the need for someone who would confirm this for me.

An Important Personality

And so, I met Foco, who was older than me. He was twenty-five years older than me. He was, and is, a well-known personality in the church. He knew the church well, had fought for the church, had known the saints, had written many biographies of saints—he was a hagiographer—he was the one who had a kind of divine plan or design not to be behind me, following, but ahead of me, helping me to understand what the Ideal was. And this then justified what I felt; that someone could tell me that it was something new. But we needed someone like him to do it.

Throughout his life—his vocation is a splendid thing—Foco had sought a virgin he could follow and bring him to God. . . . And for me too, in front of him, only twenty-eight years old, like a child . . . he was such an important personality, and I was just a provincial girl. But none of this made much impression on me. What impressed me was the beauty of Foco's soul.

He came up to see us, to meet me in Fiera di Primiero, where I was with the *pope* in that mountain cabin.

A Special Pact

One day, Foco called me aside; he felt called to say this to me: "Listen, I want to become a saint. So, I want to bind myself tightly, as Saint Catherine says, and so I would like to make a vow of obedience to you, Chiara. Because I have the impression that God has chosen you, and all of my life I have sought a virgin to be able to follow her. And I think I have found her. I want to do your will, Chiara, and I think it is God's will that I do so." He said, "In this way, Chiara, we will become saints."

I listened, but I didn't like the idea. Something within me reacted negatively to the idea. I had two feelings together.

One said, "Here Foco is under the action of a grace; we shouldn't waste this grace." The other feeling said, "No, not just two of us. All should be one, not just two being one. That, 'all might be one' (Jn 17:21), not two might be one.... And I didn't understand the part about obedience either. I said: "A vow to me? Why? One with me and with everyone. Why obedience to me?"

So I said to Foco, "Look, it might be that what you feel is really from God. But not two one, all one. But it may really be that it is from God so we shouldn't waste it.... You know my life, it is to be nothing, because I live Jesus Forsaken, and so I exist if I am nothing. He is everything, I am the nothingness. So, if I want to be what I truly am, I have to be nothing, and in this way I exist. And you are nothing, because you too are Jesus Forsaken. We have to live this nothingness. If we are this nothingness, then we are what we are, because we put ourselves in our true being. As Saint Catherine said: 'I am nothing, you are Everything.'"

So I said, "Let's do this. Tomorrow, when we go to Mass and there, when Jesus-Eucharist enters into me and when Jesus-Eucharist enters into you, he will enter into an empty chalice because there is nothing there. So we, who are nothing, will say to him ... I will say, 'Jesus, make unity with Jesus-Eucharist in him, and bring about that unity that you want with [Foco's] soul.'"

So, we went to the church, to Mass, and at Communion, Jesus entered our heart. At Communion I really made this pact and said to Jesus: "On the nothingness of me, which I am, I ask you to make this pact of unity with you on the nothingness of Foco who is there."

In the Bosom of the Trinity

We left the church. Foco had to go back in through the sacristy to give a talk to the Capuchin Fathers. I felt urged to return to the church itself. I entered the church and went in front of the tabernacle. And, in front of the tabernacle I was about to begin a prayer to Jesus-Eucharist, beginning, "Jesus . . ." But I couldn't say it because Jesus was here. I too was him. It was me. I was one with him. I was him. I couldn't call myself. And I found myself as a person on the peak of a very, very high mountain, as though I was on a very fine point, fine like a needle. And one.

So [I was on] a very high mountain, but incapable of calling out to the one who I was. The Eucharist doesn't call out to itself. And there I heard a word emerge from my mouth: "Father."

And in that moment, I found myself in the bosom of the Most Holy Trinity.

You might ask me: "How did it happen? What did you see?" It was as if I had entered into an immense abyss, like the universe, but even greater. I saw it, not with these eyes, but with the eyes of the soul. I almost didn't have these eyes, didn't have these eyes. And to the eyes of my soul it appeared to be all made of gold, all flames. And I found myself there. And I realized that the one who had put the word *"Abba, Father"* on my lips had been the Holy Spirit. And that Jesus-Eucharist, the bond of unity, had been truly the bond of unity between me and Foco. And that he alone remained on these two nothingnesses. And that our two rays had arrived at the point where they converge in the sun. And it was as if I had arrived in this infinite sun. And that outside of me had remained created reality. And I understood that I had entered into the uncreated: into God, into the bosom of the Father. I didn't see what was in Paradise. I couldn't distinguish anything, but this did not disturb me. It was infinite, but I felt very much at home.

Foco came out from his meeting with the Fathers. "Come," I said to him. We went around the church and walked over and sat on a bench. I said, "Listen to what happened to me. Do you know where we are?" And I explained. Foco listened.

Then I went home. And I loved the *pope*. And the *pope* had followed me to that point, and I wanted to tell them everything. So I gathered them together and told them. I said what was happening to me and what I saw. I said, "Listen, come with us. On your own tomorrow, ask Jesus-Eucharist in you to make the pact of unity on the nothingness of you with Jesus-Eucharist in me and in Foco."

—Donald Mitchell, ed., *Paradise*, 73–79

Resurrection of Rome

After the experience of Paradise '49, Chiara Lubich returned from the mountains. Here, she offers a meditation written in October of 1949 on the meaning of everyday urban life in the light of the new experience of God-love, and what it would mean for her and those who followed this way to return from the heights of the Dolomites to the city.

If I look at this city of Rome as it is, my Ideal seems far away. It appears to me as distant as the days in which the saints and martyrs illuminated everything around them with that eternal light which reached even the walls of these monuments that still stand in witness of the love that united the first Christians.

In blatant contrast, today's world, with all its filth and vanities, dominates this city's streets and even more so the hidden recesses of every home where anger, every kind of sin and uneasiness lurk. I would say my Ideal was a utopia if I did not think of Him, who also saw a world like this one. He was surrounded by it and at the end of his life appeared to be swept up by it, overcome by evil.

He too gazed upon the crowds around him whom he loved as himself, whom he created. He wanted to forge the bonds that would unite them to him, like children to a father, and unite them to one another as brothers and sisters.

He came down from heaven to reunite us as family: to make us all one. He came with words filled with Fire and Truth that burned through the accumulation of vanities that cover the life of the Eternal that lives in every person and that passes among them. And yet, notwithstanding, people, many people, though understanding, did not want to understand and remained with lifeless eyes because their souls were in darkness.

And all this because he made them free.

He who descended from heaven to earth could have resurrected them all with a single glance. But, because they had been created in the image and likeness of God, he had to let them experience the joy of freely conquering heaven. Eternity was at stake. They would have the opportunity to live as children of God for all eternity, like God, creators of their own happiness (because participants in the omnipotence of God).

He looked at the world as I see it now, but he did not doubt.

Unsatisfied and sad as he watched everything going to ruin, he responded by praying at night to the heavens above and the heaven within, there where the Trinity lived, the true being, everything, while outside along the streets there was only emptiness that passes.

And I too follow his example so as never to separate myself from the Eternal, from the Uncreated, which is the root of creation and therefore the Life of all, in order to believe in the ultimate victory of Light over darkness.

I pass through Rome, and I do not want to look at it.

I look at the world within me, and I cling to all that has being and value. I become completely one with the Trinity that lives in my soul, allowing myself to be enlightened by its eternal Light and filled with its heaven. I live in that heaven populated by the angels and saints who, not being constrained by the limits of time and space, can all convene in a unity of love with the Three in my humble being.

And I make contact with the Fire that, having invaded the depths of my humanity given to me by God, makes me another Christ, another God-Man by participation. Thus, my humanity merges with the divine and my eyes are no longer lifeless. Instead, through the pupil, which is the emptiness of my soul through which all the Light within me passes (if I let God live in me), I look at the world and everything in it. But it is no longer I; it is Christ in me who looks at the world and desires to make the blind see, the mute speak, and the crippled walk. They are those blinded to the vision of God living within them and outside them; mute to the Word of God that also speaks within them and that could be communicated in turn to others, reawakening the Truth in them. They are the crippled who are unable to move, because they ignore the divine will that from the depths of their hearts spurs them on to an eternal motion that is eternal Love, for when we transmit Fire we are set ablaze.

Therefore, opening my eyes once again to the world outside, I see humanity with the eyes of God who believes all things because he is Love.

I see and I discover my same Light in others, the true Reality of myself, my true self in them (perhaps hidden or secretly camouflaged out of shame). And, having found myself, I reunite myself to me, resurrecting myself in my brother or sister—because Love is Life.

Jesus is resurrected in them; another Christ, another God-Man, manifestation here on earth of the Father's goodness and the Eye of God on humanity. Thus, I extend the Christ in me to my brother or sister and I form a living and complete cell of the Mystical Body of Christ: a living cell, a hearth of God that possesses Fire and Light, which must be communicated.

It is God who makes two persons one by placing himself third, as the relationship between them: Jesus among us.

Thus, love circulates and naturally carries with it (because of its innate law of communion), like a blazing river, all that the two possess to the point that all their material and spiritual goods are held in common.

All this gives concrete and outward witness to a love that is unitive, to true love, the love that comes from the Trinity.

Therefore, the complete Christ truly lives again in both persons, in each one and among us.

He, the God-Man, in the most varied human expressions imbued with the divine, placed at the service of the eternal design: God concerned with his kingdom, ruler of all, distributor of every good thing to all his children like a father who shows no preferences.

And I think that if I allow God to live in me and if I allow him to love himself in those around me, he would discover himself in many of them, and many eyes would light up with his Light: a tangible sign that he reigns in them.

And his Fire, which destroys everything in the service of eternal Love, would spread like lightning throughout Rome resurrecting Christians and making this era, cold because atheistic, the era of Fire, the era of God.

But it is important that we have the courage not to waste too much time in other activities that simply reawaken a little Christianity, trying to echo past glories; or at least we should not give them the same priority.

We need to allow God to be reborn within us and keep him alive. We need to make him overflow onto others like torrents of Life and resurrect the dead.

And keep him alive among us by loving one another (and to love it is not necessary to make a lot of noise: love is dying to ourselves—and death is silence—and life in God—and God is the silence that speaks).

So everything is renewed: politics and art, school and religion, private life and entertainment. Everything.

The presence of God in us is not like a crucifix that hangs on the wall of a classroom as nothing more than a talisman. He is alive in us—if we let him live—as the legislator of every human and divine law, since he made them all. And from the most intimate recesses of our being he dictates them one by one. He, the eternal Teacher, teaches us what is eternal and what is passing and gives value to everything.

But only those who let Christ live in them, and therefore they themselves live in those around them, can understand this. Because life is love and if it does not circulate it does not live.

Jesus needs to be resurrected in the Eternal City and introduced everywhere. He is Life, the fullness of Life. He is not just a religious event....[2] This attempt to separate

---

2. It is sometimes thought that the gospel does not resolve all human problems and that it brings about the kingdom of God understood solely in a religious sense. But this is not so. Certainly it is not the historical Jesus or Jesus as Head of the Mystical Body who resolves all problems. This is done by Jesus-us, Jesus-me, Jesus-you.... It is Jesus in human beings, in each particular human being, when his grace is in them, who builds a bridge, opens the road. Jesus is the true, deepest personality of each individual. Every human being (every Christian), in fact, is more

him from the entirety of our lives is a practical heresy of today's world. It subjects men and women to something that is beneath them and relegates God the Father far from his children.³

No, he is the Man, the perfect man, who sums up and contains all men and women and every truth and inspiration that they may feel in order to raise themselves to their proper place.

Therefore, the one who has found this man has found the solution to every problem, be it human or divine. It is enough to love him.

—Lubich, *Essential Writings*, 173–76

Foundation of the Gen Movement

Here Chiara reflects on how the new spirituality or charism of unity is lived not just by adults but especially by the youth. The experience of the youth in its context has its own integrity and radical form of existence.

Along with the geographical spreading of the Ideal of Unity, as years passed, the structures of the Movement were

---

a child of God (= another Jesus) than a child of his or her own parents. It is as another Christ, member of his Mystical Body, that each person makes a specific and personal contribution in every field: science, art, politics.... It is the incarnation that continues, a full incarnation that involves all of the Jesuses of the Mystical Body of Christ.

3. Humanity, in all of its human dimensions and capacities, is not to be mortified but elevated. Next to a renewed theology, "new" (because it is based on the trinitarian life lived in the Mystical Body of Christ), there also needs to be new science, new sociology, new art, new politics—new because they are of Christ, renewed by his Spirit. We need to set in motion a new humanism, where humanity is really at the center, that humanity which before all else is Christ and Christ in human beings.

also developing. Here too, seemingly secondary incidents inspired new projects and new foundations.

Chiara had a particular love for the younger generations because she looked forward to passing the flag on to them. To her, they seemed just as radical and enthusiastic as those young people—all of them young women—who had begun the adventure in Trent. "You've stolen my heart," she one day told the Gen 3 (young teenage members of the Movement). Right from the start, the young children always seemed to find it easier to understand and live the words of Jesus than did the adults. Even at the early Mariapolises in Primiero there were many children. On August 20, 1962, Chiara was walking under a starry sky with some companions near the Marian Shrine of Einsiedeln in Switzerland. Gazing toward the Milky Way she said, "New generations will be born: a first, second, third, and fourth. . . ."

Vincenzo Eletto Folonari served as a guide for these young people. Following his death on July 12, 1964, Chiara wrote in her diary: "Let's hope that something will come from this suffering, something for them [the children] in the heart of the Work of Mary, something for the glory of God, something to make the Church more beautiful. After all, Eletto would have desired nothing else."

* * * * *

In the latter half of the 1960s, young people across the Western world were in deep turmoil, manifesting their unease with forms of protest that exploded in American and European student and university circles, leading in turn to a wider movement of dissent that eventually culminated in the so-called 1968 riots. Through an awareness dating back to 1949, which could be summarized by the maxim "my I is humanity," Chiara understood the sense of disillusion felt by the younger generations in the 1960s. Her intuition to invest in them dates to 1962.

Appreciating young people's desire to be heard, interpreting their profound search for authenticity and the meaning of life, understanding their need for being protagonists, foreseeing the imminent manifestation of largescale youth protests and conflicts between the generations, Chiara called together numerous young people who shared the spirituality of unity. She entrusted them with the task of launching a peaceful revolution in the world, based on Gospel love and the slogan—which sympathetically paraphrased the appeal made in the closing paragraphs of the *Communist Party Manifesto* of Marx and Engels of 1848—"Young people of the whole world, unite!" In the spring of 1967, the Gen (New Generation) Movement was born, and its first international meeting was celebrated with the symbolic gesture of passing a flag from the first to the second generation of the Movement. On either side of that flag were printed the same program and secret for making unity a reality. On one side: "That they may all be one" (Jn 17:21); and on the other: "My God, my God, why have you forsaken me" (Mt 27:46).

—Maurizio Gentilini, *Chiara Lubich*, 110

* * * *

If we, Father, were truly to look to the glory of God and the possibility of gathering for Him the greatest number possible, we should seek among the little ones to spread the Ideal, for there our work would produce the most.

Look, Father, at your hundred and fifty children and see them as a most precious mine from which can be drawn out so much glory for God; and do not see them only as children, but as souls like ours, better than ours, and speak to them—when you feel urged from within—about our Ideal.

You will see how they understand it! I always say that I love to be among children because they are the ones who best understand my Ideal.

—Chiara Lubich, *Amatevi*, 19

* * * *

I was asked, "Who are the Gen 4 [children ages four to eight] for you?"

You Gen 4 are like the buds of a tree. Do you see?

There are little buds on a tree. There are little buds on a tree, and you are like the little buds on a tree. From the buds come forth little leaves, then come forth flowers, then come forth . . . the fruit. . . . Note the flowers, then the little leaves fill themselves out, you see, the flowers here and the fruits there—red, orange, and yellow.

So, you are the little buds; however, if there are no little buds . . . it is impossible for the little leaves to come out, for the flowers to come out, for the fruits to come out.

And who are the little leaves? The little leaves are the Gen 3, and there are many, as you heard yesterday, there are so many . . . Gen 3; the little flowers are the Gen 2, and the fruits are the adults, the big people, but everything comes from the buds.

So who are you? You are something precious, very precious: you ensure that the tree will flourish. You are very precious. So, this is what you are to me!

Now let us take a look at a tree. . . . I have seen them over the last few months in my garden, where there were these delicate, delicate little buds, from which there grow leaves, flowers, fruit. The little buds, they produce everything, they produce everything.

So you too are the hope of the Movement because the tree is the whole Movement, with the Gen 4, the Gen 3, the Gen 2, on up to the adults.

> —Chiara Lubich to the Gen 4, children of the Focolare Movement, Castel Gandolfo (Rome), June 18, 1988, in *Archivio Generale Movimento dei Focolari* (AGMF), Archivio Chiara Lubich (ACL), Section 5, Talks and Conversations—unpublished document—official translation by the Focolare Communication Office/Linguistic Services (COM-SL).

The Family Is Our Future

Address to Nineteenth International Congress for the Family, Lucerne, Switzerland (May 16, 1999)

I would like to stop for a moment to reflect on the family as seen in the mind of God. Certainly it is a bold proposal but not an impossible one. It is enough to look for the answer in the Bible, the book that relates his words and the history of his relationship with humankind. It is also not a useless proposal, because besides shedding light on the often confusing and contradictory state of affairs of the family today, such a study might also help us to understand what the family is meant to be.

The family's natural beauty—The Bible is interwoven with nuptial analogies and familial symbols. It is as if the Spirit could not find another way to express the ardor, faithfulness, gratuitousness, and universality of the love of God. And it is also a confirmation that also natural marriage, as God imagined it, has in some way a sacred character.

At the beginning of creation there is a man and a woman.

God entrusts them with the commandment of mutual love, and he invites them to multiply and to use all created things. It is a beautiful image; it is the discovery of the existence of the other and the birth of the family. Human beings are called to live in relationship with one another. It is how they fulfill themselves. *"Amo ergo sum"* (I love therefore I am), writes Emmanuel Mounier.[4]

It is a "relational" dimension that encompasses all aspects of human life: family, surroundings, and history. And in this "being in relationship" we find yet another confirmation that the family is an intrinsic part of the human person; it is part of our very nature. It is not a form of living together based on a given social model or invented by a dominant group.

Conjugal communion is based on the natural complementarity between a man and a woman, which in matrimony is expressed in the total giving of self. It is a gift exclusive to and typical of conjugal union, in which the two do not simply give something of themselves, they give themselves, to the point of becoming one. It is a course mapped out by the laws of nature, but that also evokes and expresses divine laws.

Moreover, in matrimony the man and the woman, each urged by love one for the other, adhere to the universal vocation to unity. According to the bishop and theologian Klaus Hemmerle, in the union of the two spouses that are made one while being open to the possibility of welcoming children, there is a simultaneous encounter with and penetration into the world by man and woman. And in this relationship between the world and humankind we can also understand each one's specific role: man's role in dedicating

---

4. Emmanuel Mounier, "Le personalisme," in *Oeuvres* (Paris: Éditions du Seuil, 1961), 455.

himself to building the world, and woman's, to the process of making it more human, which, in fact, is her typical characteristic. But there is more.

Its trinitarian roots—The family is indissolubly intertwined with the very mystery of the life of God that is Unity and Trinity: "God created humankind in his image, in the image of God he created them; male and female he created them. God blessed them, and God said to them, 'Be fruitful and multiply, and fill the earth'" (Gn 1:27–28).

And when someone asked Jesus to speak about marriage he quoted precisely this passage from Genesis, and he recommended that they go back to how it was "in the beginning" if they wanted to understand something about the mystery of married love.

Therefore, when God created humankind, he formed a family. He created a man and a woman called to live in communion, in the image of the mystery of love of his very being. He called them to be fertile and to make use of all created things in the image of God's inexhaustible paternity. John Paul II affirms: "In the light of the New Testament it is possible to discern how the primordial model of the family is to be sought in God himself, in the trinitarian mystery of his life. The divine 'We' is the eternal pattern of the human 'we,' especially of that 'we' formed by the man and the woman created in the divine image and likeness."[5]

It is precisely here that the family plants its roots.

Certainly, the mystery of love encompasses all of creation. The laws of nature are the laws of love, and human love sums up and refines this continuous dynamic of unity and distinction.

Protector of life and treasure chest of relationships of love—

---

5. Letter to families, in *Insegnamenti di Giovanni Paulo II*, 1964, vol. XVII, no. 1 (Vatican City, 1996), 261.

Human love has its seasons. It begins when the couple falls in love. It is like a spark of the love of God that ignites the life of a family. Or like a bolt of lightning that lights up the persons loved with a new light, a novelty that changes their lives, that gives joy and enthusiasm as they set out together on a journey with no end in sight. It is almost a couple's genetic inheritance.

Then comes the fruit-bearing season, a time of growth and consolidation. Situations change, people themselves over time change and evolve. Love experiences other moments, other flavors, and other expressions, and so our capacity to love must continuously be renewed.

Precisely in this dynamic, which makes them into a one that cannot be dissolved, is contained the couple's entire future. And it is a future that leads them beyond themselves, in particular through the birth of children. In fact, fecundity among spouses has multiple expressions, the most typical being the blossoming of new human life.

In procreation the spouses cooperate with the creative action of God who through them extends his earthly family. Bonhoeffer writes: "He (God) allows men and women to participate in his continuous creative act. Parents welcome children as gifts from God and must lead them back to him."[6] In a certain sense, the birth of a baby is the typical way for a married couple to give God to the world.

Parenthood is an important stage of a family's development. It is the birth and multiplication of new relationships, a phenomenon that will increase as the life of the family progresses. The family will become a treasure chest, a wonderful interweaving of relationships of love, of intimacy, and of friendship: nuptial love among the spouses, mater-

---

6. From a sermon in the military prison of Berlin, on the occasion of a wedding, 1943.

nal and paternal love toward the children, filial love toward the parents, brotherly and sisterly love among the children, love on the part of grandparents for their grandchildren and vice versa, for aunts and uncles, for cousins, for friends of the family, for neighbors. . . . God truly created the family as a mysterious jewel interlaced with love.

—Lubich, *Essential Writings*, 185–87

Toward a New Humanity

Address to the New Humanity Movement Congress, Rome (March 20, 1983)

We know . . . that although we try, with the best of intentions, to improve the conditions of human life and to give the greatest possible assistance to others, our efforts are not always successful. The fact is that, notwithstanding all our good intentions, we are human and we soon experience our limitations. Often we are tempted to give up, either because of our personal inadequacy or due to external factors. We begin to feel indifferent, or decide to leave things as they are, or else shut ourselves off from everything else and consider only our own needs.

Why does this happen? It happens because we often believe that we have to struggle ahead on our own, relying on our own strength alone.

This is where our New Humanity Movement comes into the picture. The specific contribution it has to offer, wherever it is, in every country where it is present, is to tell the world—through concrete experiences—that when it comes to the immense undertaking of renewing society, of giving it new hope and confidence, and offering it genuine, adequate and lasting goods, we are not alone.

As we know, our Movement came about because a small group of people, a microcosm of humanity, discovered a "wellspring," and let themselves be imbued by a stream of living water, that is, by a new and deeper understanding of the good news that God is Love!

God loves us. God loves everyone.

In our lives, even in the everyday circumstances of life, with its problems and projects, its sufferings and joys, we are not alone. If we so desire, and if we are open to it, the presence of God, this extraordinary presence of a higher being, can play a role in all that we do, helping us in unexpected ways, and enriching and ennobling each and every aspect of our daily lives.

We have a Father, and his divine providence follows what we are doing and watches over us.

Certainly, this faith in God's love is present, even today, in the hearts of many. Nonetheless, we often fail to perceive the logical consequences of this faith. We put all our effort into building up the "earthly" city, with the desire of renewing the world, but we act as if we had to do it all on our own.

Our New Humanity Movement wants to rekindle, both in its own members and in as many other people as possible, the awareness of the truth that God is on our side, and since we do indeed have a Father in heaven, he will give us our "daily bread," along with everything else we need, as Igino Giordani affirmed.[7]

I will give you just one example. Throughout its forty years of life, one of the strongest convictions that our Movement has developed, one that is supported by our daily experiences, is that living the Good News and launching the

---

7. See Igino Giordani, *Il messaggio sociale del cristianesimo* (Rome: Città Nuova Editrice, 1960), 41; *Il messaggio sociale di Gesù* (Rome: Città Nuova Editrice, 1951), 109–13.

revolution of the Gospel in the world is synonymous with launching the most powerful social revolution possible.

Is there social inequality in the world today?

Are the rich and the poor still on opposite fronts?

We believe, as Mary did, that the law of the Gospel put into practice can truly fill the hungry with good things and send "the rich away empty" (Lk 1:53). And through the grace of God we have seen this fulfilled in many places all over the world.

We can attest to the fact that if the beatitude on poverty (see Lk 6:20) and Jesus's warning, "Woe to you who are rich" (Lk 6:24), are taken seriously, they can give a powerful thrust to the restoration of social equality.

Are we faced with concerns about care for the elderly, the unemployed, the marginalized, people with disabilities, those who are starving, and all the many problems of the developing nations?

Doesn't the whole history of Christianity tell us that we can find incredible solutions by living what will be the "final exam" for every Christian: "I was hungry and you gave me food . . ." (Mt 25:35)? Haven't we ourselves also experienced that by putting that page of the Gospel into practice, without compromising, responding to the needs of our day and using methods suited to the times, many of these problems can be resolved?

We know that the Gospel requires us to "give" ("Give, and it shall be given to you") and that it also promises that we will receive a "good measure pressed down, shaken together, running over" (Lk 6:38), which is something that our Movement has experienced many times. But isn't this also a very practical, concrete way of acting, capable of relieving those who suffer from poverty, hunger, and loneliness, and are in need of everything?

It is also our daily experience that in "asking" as the Gospel teaches, we receive (see Lk 11:10). It says that "all these things will be given to you as well" (Mt 6:33), and "these things" could be health for some people or a job for others, or a home, or a child, or some other necessity for others.

We have often seen with our own eyes, to the glory of God, the "hundredfold" that Christ promised to those who have left everything to follow him (see Mt 19:27). We have counted them—and all of you here can testify to this, too! We have "hundreds" of brothers and sisters, an endless number of true brothers and sisters with whom we form one family, with all the spiritual and material consequences that that implies. We have "hundreds" of houses in the various parts of the world where our Movement has spread. Every day we personally experience providence of all sorts that arrives without fail.

And if we receive it, because of doing our small part, with the grace of God, and because of giving the little love we have, why can't it happen everywhere? Is there division in the world? Is the arms race still on? Are there wars and terrorism?

Who can deny that evangelical love would be the best guarantee of peace? Living this kind of love means loving every neighbor—literally—loving one's neighbor as oneself and loving one's enemy. This is the characteristic of Christianity. It also means practicing the New Commandment, which is the precious pearl of the Gospel. In fact, loving one another on a vast scale, among all people, would be the best antidote for all the grave evils and tremendous dangers that plague the world today.

Do we have to deal with problems of drug addiction, burglaries, and theft? Do we see around us evidence of pornography and violence? We can ask why human beings stoop to such levels? It's because they are seeking happiness.

We who are sincerely trying to live our Christian faith know from long experience that the evangelical adventure of love, which means living our lives for others, indeed "living the life of the others," is the source of immense, genuine happiness. Let's help as many people as possible to take delight in the fullness of joy that Jesus promised. If we do so, many of these sad incidents will disappear. What has done more to save and rebuild our families than putting into practice the words of Christ, "What God has joined together, let no one separate" (Mt 19:6)?

And hasn't the image of Mary, presented in the Gospel as the noblest of all created beings, always been for us the unparalleled justification of the role of women? Then why can't she give similar inspiration to many other people, too? Have people lost sight of the fact that they all belong to an organized society, a community, and therefore share in its rights and responsibilities? It has been our experience that the observance of the words "Give to Caesar what is Caesar's" (Mt 22:21) is truly the most effective guarantee that the laws of the state will be obeyed—as long as they are not opposed to the laws of God.

All this and more convince us that our life on earth, which is frequently so monotonous and difficult, can change course and take flight.

It's not impossible for us to dream of something that few people today dare to acknowledge: that the world *can* change and that, contrary to the decadence we see around us, the world is heading toward a new era.

Together with all those who seek the good of humanity, we want this to be our characteristic contribution to the renewal of the world; that is, we want to offer people the experience of living the gospel, with all its repercussions on our individual and social life here on earth. We want to offer this experience in every country where we are present: in our homes and offices, in schools, factories, and legislatures, in our communities, our meetings, our centers, and our little towns.

We want to offer this experience all together. We come from a variety of nations, and represent different races, nationalities, and languages, and yet it is possible for us to live in love and harmony, to have peace and happiness reign among us, and to lack nothing that we need. And so why can't this be true for many, many other people, too?

Today we will speak about concrete endeavors. In describing them, we will use terms such as labor, unemployment, voluntarism, legislative measures, international law, and so forth.

What we want to affirm at the outset is that if these small-scale endeavors, or larger individual or collective experiences, can renew humanity, they are not merely the result of our personal efforts or of the particular talents that some of us might have. Rather, they are the fruit of our wanting to put into practice whatever we have understood of the Gospel, wherever in the world God has placed us.

There is a particular truth, a truth of the Gospel that the Holy Spirit has called to our attention in a special way, from the very beginning of the Movement. It is a truth we are called to fulfill with the utmost commitment, an evangelical truth which affirms that whenever we are united in the name of Christ, he is present among us (see Mt 18:20). Therefore, he is not only present in the tabernacles of our churches, and not only in the people who have been called to proclaim his message or to govern his Church. No. He is also present among all of us, in the midst of us, his people.

This is the exciting truth that tells us he did not just pass through the world twenty centuries ago and remain only a few years. On the contrary, as the risen Lord, he is present in our midst each time we love one another as he wants us to, sharing one another's hopes, aspirations, needs, sufferings, struggles, and achievements. He is present according to his astounding promise: "And remember, I am with you always, until the end of the age" (Mt 28:20).

Why do we want to stress this particular passage of the Gospel? Is this presence of Jesus important? Yes, it's very important! It's indispensable, especially for us who are members of the New Humanity Movement. We who have been called to build up the earthly city must, in a certain sense, continue the work of the Creator.

Now, to whom did the Father look when he created the universe? The Gospel says: "In the beginning was the Word.... All things came to being through him" (Jn 1:1–3). Through him, through the Word, all things came into being.

Therefore, the Word had a role to play in creation. The plan for humankind and for creation was summed up in him. When the Father created the universe, he saw his plan in the Word.

We who want to contribute to the renewal of the world, to whom should we look for guidance in building up the earthly city in a harmonious way, and as a continuation of the work of the Creator?

Who can best enlighten us? Jesus, the Incarnate Word. We need to look at him, and this will be easier if he is present in our midst.

No one better than Jesus will be able to suggest to us what we should do, to support us in the work that we have already undertaken, to correct us or give us the courage to start all over again.

But the presence of Jesus in our midst is important for another reason as well. We know that as human beings we carry within ourselves an incurable wound, because we long for the supernatural life. The divine torments us; the infinite haunts us; the eternal attracts us.

We know that even if we succeeded in renewing the whole of humankind, and actually building a new world, our hearts would not yet have attained all they yearn for. Why? Because we have been made for a life that never ends. Thus we must stress here yet another truth. In building the earthly city, we can begin right now to construct something that will not pass away, because we can contribute, with our efforts and with our work, to the coming of the "new heavens" and the "new earth" (2 Pt 3:13) that await us.

In fact, in redeeming the universe, Christ also redeemed all human activity. Indeed, he redeemed every human project as well. The universe will not be annihilated, but rather transformed. There will be no rupture between this world and the next, but rather there will be continuity.

The good fruits of nature and of our industriousness (in other words, what we accomplish day by day) will not disappear. On the contrary, we will find them again, purified, enlightened, and transformed (see *Gaudium et spes*, §39).

This is a truth that makes your soul exalt! It is a consoling and sublime vision of our calling to transform the earth through our own labor. But this will only come about under one condition. Our works will remain if they have been carried out in this world according to the commandment of love (see *Gaudium et spes*, §38).

And who will guarantee that our work is being carried out in this way? Who will tell us that we are truly building on the rock of love, thus assuring us that what we are doing will not perish? It will be Jesus in our midst. Jesus in our midst who raises up every society, big or small, who makes it a cell of the earthly city and of the heavenly city as well.

He will give us this guarantee. In fact, he is fully present wherever love is alive. His presence is a gift of God and, at the same time, the fruit of our mutual charity, that charity on which we must base all of our activities. Jesus in the midst! The plan for a new humanity lies in him, and in him lies the guarantee that what we do will remain.

Dear brothers and sisters, all my dear friends, how can we not see as fascinating the path we are following, the way that stretches out before us? How can we not dream of a New Humanity, when we have here with us the one whose Spirit has said: "See, I am making all things new!" (Rev 21:5)?

—Chiara Lubich at the New Humanity International Congress, "Towards a New Humanity," Rome, March 20, 1983, published in *Città Nuova* 27, no. 7 (1983): 23–29, and in *Living City*, New York, September 1983, 2–20

2

GOING TO GOD TOGETHER

Introduction

The writings in this chapter deal with "Going to God Together." The phrase derives from Piero Coda's introduction to La dottrina spirituale *(the English edition is called* Essential Writings*). Coda's key heading, "Going to God Together, the Trinity and Mutual Love," shows the close relationship between our journey and God's gift of divine love.*

The "together" in this title does not connote pure collectivism or a merely social mode of salvation. We go "together" in the sense of being joined together in our individual missions by Christ and in Christ. We are thus still invited as distinct and diverse persons of faith to engage and enter into what Chiara Lubich took to be the basic building blocks of the charism of unity:

- *Jesus Forsaken*
- *Jesus in Our Midst*
- *Living the Gospel*
- *Mary Desolate*
- *Eucharist*

What binds these five signature realities of faith together? The trinitarian experience of God is the source of their unity. These themes in the distinct articulation and as a configuration are the essential aspects of the spiritual vision of Chiara Lubich throughout her whole life.

I Know Only Christ and Christ Crucified

Jesus Forsaken in Paradise

We had been trying with great intensity to live the main points of our spirituality: the present moment, mutual love, the Word of God. We had been trying to become identified with the Word of God with which we made our communion constantly in the present moment.

There were three compulsory communions for us: with Jesus in the Eucharist, with our brother or sister, with the Word of God. For about five years we had been meditating in our life upon the Word of Scripture and, in the spring of 1949, I realized that the effects in our life of its various words were more or less the same, if not exactly the same, as if the substance of each word were "love."

For years we had thought that, just as the whole of Jesus is in the Sacred Host and likewise in each piece of it, so also the whole of Jesus is in the Gospel and likewise in each Word of it, in each complete idea. But now we were experiencing this. As a consequence, the desire to continue this practice was gradually fading in me, not because it was not useful or out of negligence, but because it had, as it were, achieved its goal.[1]

---

1. Saying this, Chiara does not mean to devalue putting the Word into practice, but simply to underline the centrality of Jesus Forsaken who, in that moment, became "Everything" for her. In a note written at a later date, taking into account the whole experience of that summer of 1949, she wrote: "It is wonderful that even the highest mystical experience we live never stops us from contemplating the Word, but urges us to live it with always greater intensity."

I do not remember the way things happened exactly, but deep within me the conviction was taking root, with the practice that went with it, that *Jesus Forsaken* effectively summed up the whole of the Gospel. And that, in loving Him, all the virtues would blossom. In Jesus Forsaken there were all sufferings, all loves, all virtues, all sins (since He had made Himself "sin") and in Him we all found ourselves in every instant of our lives. He was the summary of physical sufferings, because he was dying, and of moral and spiritual sufferings.

He was the summary of all loves: He was "father" for having regenerated us; He was "mother" in the labor pains of our divine birth; He was brother, friend. He was the summary of the virtues: *the pure one*, to the point of being detached from every divine consolation, He who was God; *the poor one*, poor of everything, even of the sense of His divinity; He was *the obedient one*, because He was losing everything in the Father, who was Authority for Him.

In fact, in that cry He appeared to us as suffering and love together.

He had made Himself "sin" for us sinners, rebellion, division, excommunication, and so forth, out of love. I don't know how to link these two terms: love and suffering that in Jesus Forsaken appeared to us to be a single thing, so that one would not exist without the other.

By living Jesus Forsaken we had come to understand that He had *made Himself nothing* and that in this *nothingness* was our life. To be like Him out of love for Him, that nothingness that we really are.

We nothing, He all.

—Donald Mitchell, ed., *Paradise*, 58–59

A Luminous Period

The event described here was recounted in more detail earlier, in Mitchell, Paradise: Reflections on Chiara Lubich's Mystical Journey, *58–86. Here she offers her meditation, "I have only one spouse on earth," which has been a focal point for the spirituality of the Movement ever since.*

We strove to live the nothingness of ourselves so that he could live in us, and the nothingness of ourselves so that he might triumph among us as well. One day in 1949, on the background of this nothingness, when receiving holy communion, loved and rediscovered as a bond of unity, Igino Giordani[2] and I asked Jesus, in the way known to him, to unite our souls.

And through a special grace we experienced what it means to be a living cell of Christ's Mystical Body. It meant being Jesus, and as him to be in the bosom of the Father. And "Abba, Father!" (Rom 8:15; Gal 4:6) sprung to our lips.

Religion, at this moment, appeared new to us. It now meant to put ourselves alongside Jesus, our brother, in loving the Father.

It was the beginning of an especially luminous period. Among other things, it seemed that God wanted to give us an intuition of some plan of his for our Movement. We also understood better many truths of the faith, particularly who Jesus Forsaken was for humanity and for creation—he who recapitulated all things in himself.

Our experience was so powerful, it made us think life would always be like that: light and heaven. But what followed instead was the reality of everyday life.

---

2. Igino Giordani, member of the Italian parliament, author, journalist, is now considered the cofounder of the Focolare Movement because of the contribution he made to it in various ways.

A Second Choice of Jesus Forsaken

It was a rude awakening, so to speak, to find ourselves back on earth. Only Jesus Forsaken gave us the strength to carry on living: Jesus Forsaken, whom we found present in the world we had to love—a world which is what it is, namely, not heaven. In making a second and more conscious choice of the One who had called us to follow him, the now well-known decision sprung from my soul:

> I have only one Spouse on earth:
> Jesus Forsaken.
> I have no God but him.
> In him is the whole of paradise with the Trinity
> and the whole of the earth with humanity.
> Therefore what is *his* is mine, and nothing else.
> And *his* is universal suffering, and therefore mine.
> I will go through the world
> seeking it in every instant of my life.
> What hurts me is *mine*.
> Mine the suffering that touches me in the present.
> Mine the suffering of the souls beside me
> (that is my Jesus).
> *Mine* all that is not peace, not joy, not beautiful,
> not lovable, not serene,
> in a word, what is not paradise.
> Because I too have *my* paradise,
> but it is the one in my Spouse's heart.
> I know no other.
> So it will be for the years I have left:
> athirst for suffering, anguish, despair,
> sorrow, exile, forsakenness, torment—
> for all that is him,
> and he is sin, hell.

In this way
I will dry up the waters of tribulation
in many hearts nearby
and, through communion
with my almighty Spouse,
in many far away.
I shall pass as a fire
that consumes all that must fall
and leaves standing only the truth.
But it is necessary to be like him:
to be him in the present moment of life.

I wrote: "He is sin, hell."[3] Evdokimov says: "The Holy Spirit no longer binds the Son to the Father, and the Son experiences the break, the abandonment; it is solitude within the Trinity, the suffering of God, God's hell."[4]

For Hans Urs von Balthasar, Jesus Forsaken is and is not hell: "The darkness of the state of sinfulness came certainly to be experienced by Jesus, in a manner that cannot be identical with what sinners (who hate God) would have to experience . . . it is nevertheless deeper and darker than that, because it happens inside the depth of the relation of the divine hypostasis, unimaginable to every creature.

"One can therefore maintain equally well that the abandonment of God in Jesus is the opposite of hell, and that it

---

3. P. Evdokimov, *La conoscenza di Dio secondo la tradizione orientale* (Rome: Paoline, 1969), 109. (Our translation.)

4. The Orthodox theologian Olivier Clément writes: "By his self-abasement, his degradation, his passion, his dying the death of the accursed, Christ accepts into himself all hell, all the death of the fallen world, even the terrible accusation of atheism: 'My God, my God, why hast thou forsaken me?'" (O. Clément, *On Human Being* [London/Hyde Park: New City Press, 2000], 146).

precisely is hell (Luther and Calvin), indeed in its extreme intensity."[5]

—Chiara Lubich, *The Cry*, 60–63

The Trinity and Jesus Forsaken

Jesus crucified!

What can we possibly say about him? How can we speak of him appropriately?

He is a human being like us, we know that. But he is God too. He is love. He came into our midst to complete a task that involves us all, personally affecting each one of us. He created us, but we have spoiled his gift, and we keep on defacing it. And so, along with life we have inherited tears, suffering, and, in the end, death, the apparent voiding of all our experience.

But we should note how he understands the human condition; he knows the tragic events of history; he takes pity on the human race and descends to the earth: he takes upon himself everything that all human beings have to undergo.

---

5. Hans Urs von Balthasar, *Theo-Drama: Theological Dramatic Theory*, vol. 4, *The Action*, trans. Graham Harrison (San Francisco: Ignatius Press, 1994), 31.

J. Ratzinger writes: "Jesus' death-cry has been recently described by Ernest Käsemann as a prayer from hell, as the erection of the first commandment in the wilderness of God's apparent absence" (J. Ratzinger, *Introduction to Christianity*, trans. J. R. Foster [New York: Seabury Press, 1990], 226).

For Patriarch Bartholomew of Constantinople, "Jesus, the incarnate Word, covered the greatest distance that lost humanity could cover. 'My God, my God, why have you forsaken me?' An infinite distancing, the supreme torment, a prodigy of love. Between God and God, between the Father and the incarnate Word, there intervenes our despair, with which Jesus is in sympathy to the end. The absence of God is precisely hell" (Patriarch Bartholomew of Constantinople, "Commentary on the Way of the Cross at the Colosseum").

God does not will men and women to be lost (see Jn 6:39); rather, he saves them.

Jesus suffers and dies for all humankind. He dies, with us and like us, and then, rises again.

It was necessary (see Mk 8:31), said Jesus when the hour of his suffering drew near.

But what was necessary? And who needed it?

He made it necessary for himself to become incarnate, to suffer and to die for us, because he is love!

This is the extraordinary vocation of the God-Man, so totally different, so opposite to what human beings normally aspire to. He came "to give his life as a ransom for many" (Mt 20:28).

It was all prearranged by the Father. Jesus submits. But as Isaiah says of the Suffering Servant, he offered himself of his own will (see Is 53:7, Vulg.): He wants the will of the Father. He wants it because he loves the Father above all.[6]

And the Father responds to that love with his own power and performs something that he had never done since the creation, namely "the new creation": the resurrection.

In the resurrection also Jesus's body, "weak" and susceptible to pain and to death, is transfigured, is glorified (see 2 Cor 13:4), made fit to ascend to the right hand of the Father.

Thus the God-Man opens the door of the Trinity to the human beings he has redeemed.

—Lubich, *The Cry*, 17–18.

Jesus in the Midst

For Chiara and for the Movement the intimate and communal presence of Jesus is always indicated by the phrase "Jesus in the midst." Here follow excerpts of a synthesis by Chiara of her four themes related to Jesus in the midst.

---

6. "But the world must recognize that I love the Father and act just as the Father has commanded. Come now, let us go" (Jn 14:31).

Chiara: In this brief talk I would like to consider with you Jesus's words: "Where two or three are gathered in my name, I am there among them" (Mt 18:20).

In the Focolare Movement we have, without a doubt, given a preeminent place to "Jesus in our midst." We know that everything we do is of value if Jesus is in our midst, and nothing is of value if Jesus is not in our midst.

The presence of Jesus among us, as we wrote in our Statutes, is for each member of the Movement "the norm of norms, the premise to every other rule." We don't go to Mass without Jesus in our midst; we don't go out to do the apostolate without Jesus in our midst; we don't go to work without Jesus in our midst.

But as I prepare to speak to you about Jesus in our midst, I sense how dry and cold the juridical expression can be—"the norm of norms, the premise to every other rule." Jesus in the midst is not just a norm or a rule, although it's true that he does precede every other rule. Jesus in our midst, Jesus in our midst is a person! The most holy and glorious person of Jesus.

For us, from the very beginning, Jesus in the midst was everything—he was life.

When the Movement first came to life, in 1943, there wasn't much talk in Catholic circles, among the faithful, about Jesus in the midst of people.

The phrase of Jesus, "Where two or three are gathered in my name, I am there among them," which we find in Matthew's Gospel, chapter 18, verse 20, was not particularly emphasized.

Now, after the Second Vatican Council has spoken about it in such an explicit way, it has become more normal for many people.

But what conditions are needed for having Jesus in the midst?

We know the answer because we have been living it for thirty-two years. We have Jesus in our midst if we are united in his name. But what does this mean? It means if we are united in him, in his will, in love which is his will, in mutual love which is the supreme will of Jesus, his commandment, in which there is unity of heart, will, and mind, if possible in all things, but certainly in matters of faith.

After these considerations, it is clear how precious the vocation of our Movement is. Through it, many people now live like this, a life that some Fathers of the Church maintained belonged to only a few. We can see that today's world that speaks so much about communion, unity, and collectivism has actually taken this idea from the Gospel and underlined it. Christianity too should present itself as a Christian community, as communion, because that's what the world is looking for today, both those who are for Christ and those who are against him.

Now I will speak of some effects of Jesus in our midst. What does Jesus in our midst do? We'll say something about our experience.

We who have had the grace of being able to live with his presence can witness to the following: Jesus in the midst gives light.

Who enlightened us regarding the phrases of the Gospel—we were just young girls, like the Gen today—so that we saw it as something completely new, revolutionary, and full of life? Jesus in our midst.

And who, then, throughout the entire history of the Movement, inspired us with those lines of light on how to organize the Movement, the various vocations, the various regions, all over the world? Jesus, Jesus in our midst is behind every step we take. And when we don't know what to do, and don't understand what is the will of God, who else do we turn to but him? We tell one another: "Come, let's put Jesus in our midst so we can understand the will of God!"

He is the light of our life, the solution to every problem we might have.

Jesus in the midst is the salvation of the Movement and the very possibility of its life in those places where the external conditions hinder its free development, either because of other religions being intolerant toward ours, or through an environment that has been dechristianized by a materialistic mentality and way of life, or through the complete absence—as in non-Christian countries—of any knowledge of Jesus. In those places our homes are our meeting places, and Jesus in the midst makes them into churches.

I remember that especially in the beginning when we began to live this spirit, each one of us felt very strongly the difference between being united and being alone without the help of unity.

When we were alone, separated from the community—not alone and united at a distance, but rather a little "down" and therefore, detached from the community—we became aware of all our personal fragility; we felt lost, bewildered. Our will was weak and unable to carry things through. We could no longer see why we had left everything to follow Jesus. The light was missing. Jesus was missing.

When we were united, instead, we felt all the strength of Jesus among us. It was as if we were all clothed in the power and blessing of heaven. We felt capable of the noblest actions for God—it was Jesus in the midst who gave us this strength! We felt we could carry out the most ardent, difficult resolutions, which we subsequently maintained, whereas before, when alone, in spite of all our good will, it was difficult to fully live up to the promises we had made to the Lord.

Before this new life began, we were convinced that it was impossible to live the Gospel in our times—because we hadn't understood it. I remember that we used to say: "But how can we live the Gospel, how can we become holy, how can we do it? St. Catherine used chains to beat herself to the point of bleeding. St. Francis threw himself in the snow at a certain point when he was tempted. Other saints fasted. But which way should we take? Which path should we follow?" It was like facing a huge wall. We didn't know from which angle to enter into the Gospel.

And then Jesus in the midst enlightened us on the simplest words of all, those that tell us to love. Then love brings light because love opens the way to understanding all the rest of the Gospel.

If, before this new life began, we were convinced that it was impossible to live the Gospel in our times, because by ourselves we were unsuccessful in doing so, afterwards in unity we saw it was possible because Jesus himself, present in our midst, explained it to us and gave us the strength to put it into practice. He gave us the strength to do it!

This was an immense discovery—to discover the Gospel—one that was rich in consequences, and caused the birth of such a vast Movement. What do we do, what do we bring to people? We help the bishops to evangelize, that's what we do.

What is the value of Jesus in the midst? I will give you a personal experience. In a warm, filial talk that I had with the then-Bishop Montini, who later became Pope Paul VI, we spoke about the way we Christians often fall into the error of misplacing values when we consider the various riches of the Church.

That brief conversation, I remember, had to do precisely with the value of Jesus in our midst, and the ideas touched on during it were something like this: "If we are united, Jesus is among us. This is something precious—more precious than any other treasure that our hearts may possess:

more than mother, father, brothers, sisters, and children. It is worth more than our house, our work, or our property; more than the works of art in a great city like Rome." This is what I said in that conversation.

"Jesus in the midst is worth more than magnificent monuments, more than rich mausoleums, more than the art, more than all the splendor of the Vatican. He is worth more than our own souls!" That's what Jesus is—worth more than our own souls!

When Jesus is in our midst it is always a celebration. If there is one thing characteristic of our meetings, both small and large, it is the fullness of joy that radiates from each person, that lights up each face. Often when you take part in one of these meetings, you find yourself asking if it's a feast day.

Yes, because Jesus in the midst of a small group, or a large number gathered together in his name, is the Jesus of celebration, Jesus of the resurrection, who now, besides living at the right hand of the Father, also lives in the little churches made up of Christians.

In every true focolare center we are certain that he is the one who decides and arranges everything. In fact, we don't feel we are doing the will of a man or a woman when we are given some task, but rather the will of Jesus in our midst. And this creates the sense of being free children of God, of obeying God [and not a human person].

Now let's take a look at the Second Vatican Council—it's important—which God willed should take place during our lifetime.

But since for us, who live in this century, it is of utmost importance to see whether the charism that moves us is in harmony with the spirit of the entire Church today, let's glance quickly through the pages of the Council texts to see whether it speaks explicitly about Jesus in the midst.

Yes, it does. Father Foresi,[7] in his book *Reaching for More*, says: "Until the Second Vatican Council, the passage in the Gospel, 'Where two or three are gathered in my name, I am there among them,' was rarely ever mentioned. If we exclude the Council of Chalcedon, we will find that throughout the whole history of the Church, even in the most solemn conciliar documents, this phrase is almost never mentioned." Even though Jesus was present. "The Second Vatican Council, however, did not produce even one document which does not underline this fundamental idea." Therefore, it has matured in the whole Church. The Holy Spirit made it grow to maturity within the whole Church. "Without a doubt we can state that this idea was the soul of the Council, especially in the Council's statement on collegiality" (see *Lumen Gentium*, c. III).

Vatican II speaks of Jesus in the midst in the Constitution on the Sacred Liturgy, then in a splendid way in the Decree on the Renewal of Religious Life, and once again in the Decree on the Apostolate of the Laity. Finally, the Council speaks about Jesus in the midst in the Decree on Ecumenism—and this is of interest to us—inviting the faithful, in order to bring about the union of Christians, to lead a life according to the Gospel—in fact, we live the Word of Life—and to use the *"consenserint"*—that is, praying together in unity—to beseech the grace of unity among members of the various Churches, because—the Council states, "where two or three"—Catholics and non-Catholics—"are gathered in my name, I am there among them" (Mt 18:20).

---

7. Chiara Lubich met Pasquale Foresi in 1954. He would become the first priest-focolarino; he developed the Movement's program of theological studies, helped compose its statutes, established its publishing house, and helped in founding its first "little city," Loppiano. She considered him a cofounder of the Movement.

Jesus in our midst, a brother among brothers and sisters, our teacher because he enlightens, guides, gives strength, light. We have no cause to envy those who lived with him in Palestine. We have him, too! We can hope for everything from this tremendous, extraordinary promise. He is the source of a divine blaze of fire wherever he is in the world, as he said: "I came to bring fire to the earth" (Lk 12:49).

On occasions such as this one, when our meeting is necessarily ecumenical because of the number of different Churches present, let's show all our gratitude to Jesus. Even though we cannot yet be united in the bread of the Eucharist—as is very often the case—he can be among us with his spiritual presence.

If we unite together with him among us, as the Fathers say, he will enlighten us about our questions and he will be the principal teacher of theological studies and the one who will ultimately bring us to the fullness of light.

We have an immense treasure: we have *the* treasure. Let's leave behind everything else to possess it. Jesus in our midst will give us heaven on earth and in the next life as well.

—Chiara Lubich to members of the Reformed Church, "Synthesis of the Four Themes on Jesus in the Midst," Rocca di Papa, Rome, May 23, 1976, published in *Città Nuova*, Rome, 20 (1978). Official translation by the Focolare Communication Office/Linguistic Services (COM-SL)

Living the Gospel

The following passage is from Chiara Lubich's reflections during the summer of 1949, explaining what led to the mystical experience of "Paradise." The footnotes, which expand on key moments in her recollections, contain her own commentary on this experience, as recounted in conversations with members of the "Abba School" (see page 177).

Five years had gone by since the Movement began, and we had already understood[8] and made our own several main points of its spirituality, such as God-Love, the will of God, seeing Jesus in our brothers and sisters, the New Commandment, Jesus Forsaken, Jesus in the midst, unity. . . .

Now, for some time, we had been focused upon the Word of Life, which we were living with a particularly special intensity.[9] The Movement had no major structures then, nor had its activities begun, so our whole commitment consisted in living the Gospel.

The Word of God entered deeply into us, so much so that it changed our mentality. The same thing also happened to those who had some kind of contact with us.

This new mentality that was taking shape manifested itself as a true divine protest against the world's way of

---

8. Since the very beginning an important aspect of my experience of the charism I had received was, for the most part, this: I did not understand things when I was with the others; I understood them first by myself, then, communicating them to the others, they were developed, expanded. It was like this also for the graces received during '49: I understood them, then I communicated them; communicating them they were illuminated still more for me, then I wrote them down. It was like that at least in the first part of '49. After that, these graces became so frequent, both day and night, that I was not able to communicate them, but I wrote them down straightaway so as not to lose them. At other times, however, I understood things only thanks to the presence of Jesus in the midst with someone.

9. It is amazing how intensely we were living the Word. The Word was our life, our very breath. We felt that we had to be the Word, that we had meaning only by being the Word. Nothing else had significance, neither circumstances, nor suffering, nor illness. . . . Everything was absorbed by the Word. Therefore in us there no longer lived Chiara, Graziella, Natalia . . . but there lived Christ who is the Word. This radical way of living made us free from every form of conditioning. We had discovered freedom in the Word.

thinking, of wanting, of acting. And it brought about a re-evangelization in us.[10]

The intensity with which we were living the Word of God at that time, then, gave us a unique experience, which has not been repeated since then in the Movement.

Living one Word and then another and yet another, we came to realize that, when putting any Word of God into practice, in the end, the effects were the same.[11] For example, living the Word: "Blessed are the pure in heart . . ." (Mt 5:8) or "Blessed are the poor in spirit . . ." (Mt 5:3) or "Blessed are the meek . . ." (Mt: 5:5) or "Love your neighbor as yourself" (Mt 22:39) or "Do not do to others what you would not have done to you" (see Tb 4:15; Mt 7:12; Lk 6:31) brought us to the same conclusion, obtained for us the same effects.

The fact is that every Word, even though expressed in human terms and in different ways, is Word of God.[12] But since God is Love (see 1 Jn 4:8, 16), every Word is charity. We believe that at that time, beneath every Word, we had discovered charity.

And when one of these Words settled into our soul, it seemed to us that it was transformed into fire, into flames;[13]

---

10. By living the Word we understood and communicated the Gospel to everyone. And it was above all thanks to the Word lived out that we won over many people. Our evangelization has always been above all by living the Word and then also proclaiming it.

11. The life of the Word, in fact, brought about in us a single effect: to be always in the supernatural because we were dead to ourselves and alive in God. And it was this intense living of the Word that made us be Jesus, individually and together, making possible our entry into Paradise.

12. In the sense that every Word, even though expressed in human terms that display different ways of dying, is God's Word.

13. Indeed, the life of the Word purified us to the point of making us experience the immense effect of feeling a spiritual fire burning within.

it was transformed into love. It could be said that our inner life was all love.[14]

This charity, moreover, amplified within us what we called "the voice." The Word lived out intensified it like a loudspeaker, so that we could distinguish it well, even among the thousand blaring sounds of the world.

As far as I recall, the last Word we had been living in that period was "My God, my God why have you forsaken me" (Mk 15:34; 27:46). And Jesus Forsaken appeared to us as the Word par excellence, the Word totally unfurled, the Word completely opened out. All that was needed, therefore, was to live him.

In that way everything was made simple. Living him meant living the nothingness of ourselves, so all of us were for God (in his will) and for the others.[15]

But other experiences of the Word were added to this.

For example, we would say that just as the whole of

---

14. We experienced it: the Word entered and it became fire, so our inner life was all love, a love that was felt, not a love that was only theoretical. And this feeling a spiritual fire within was a special grace, a mystical experience that we were already living before entering Paradise.

15. What I say here is important: "Living him (Jesus Forsaken) meant living the nothingness of ourselves." As we will see, indeed, when we sealed the pact with Foco we asked Jesus-Eucharist that he seal a pact of unity between us "on the nothingness of ourselves"; we did not ask: "on our mutual love." But "on the nothingness of ourselves" means "on our mutual love," because "living him" is precisely "living the nothingness of ourselves in order to be all for God and for the others." Moreover, to live Jesus Forsaken it is necessary to live the will of God. The will of God, indeed, is synonymous with living Jesus Forsaken because living it we put our own will to death, just as, in any case, loving the other is synonymous with loving Jesus Forsaken. Jesus said "my food is to do the will of God" (see Jn 4:34), and not that the will of God is his law or his style of life. Food makes us live and grow. And when we love Jesus Forsaken or the will of God we no longer live for ourselves, but God lives in us and therefore we grow.

Jesus is in the Sacred Host and in each of its fragments, so the whole of Jesus is in the Gospel and in each of its Words.[16]

Later we seemed to understand that in the Word is present, in a certain way, Jesus, dead and risen. He is present dead in the negative part of the Word and risen in the positive.[17]

—Unpublished document, *Paradise '49*, paragraphs 1–14. Used with permission of the Focolare Office for Wisdom and Study

---

16. Understanding that the whole of Jesus is in the Gospel and that he is also in each of its Words is a vision from the bosom of the Trinity, where we already were by grace—hence we were there even before our entry into the Father. In the same way, to understand that the whole of Jesus is in the Sacred Host and in each of its fragments is a trinitarian vision. The fact that the whole of Jesus is present in each Word of his shows, furthermore, that just as in each of the spiritualities, which center on a single word (for example "unity" for us, "poverty" for the Franciscans), there is contained the whole of the Gospel. It is necessary, therefore, to find him in each word and live him. And we can find him by basing our lives on love. It is loving, in any case, that generates true poverty. Indeed, charity is the mother of all the virtues. Now, bringing love into the other religious families means bringing about their rebirth. And this is the gift we give them.

17. Intensely living the Word, I had observed, as I will say later in these pages, that in it there is always a negative part—for example: "Blessed are the poor in spirit"—and a positive part—"for theirs is the kingdom of heaven" (Mt 5:3); even though it may seem that one of these two aspects is lacking, nonetheless that aspect is implicit. It seemed to me I understood that in every Word there is the presence of Jesus, dead and risen: in the negative part of the Word is present and expressed the death of Jesus; in the positive, his resurrection. And, in fact, the very existence of Jesus, entirely lived out in total love for the Father and for human beings, was all death and resurrection: the expression and revelation on earth of the non-being and being of the love within the Trinity. The same reality therefore is in his Word, in each one of his Words. And the same reality is present and manifested in the existence of whoever lives the Word, and so in the life of the Church.

Mary Desolate

From an Address to the Focolare Movement's Study Group on the Media and Communications (June 6, 2000)

Three years ago we focused on the terrible and fascinating mystery of the cry of Jesus crucified: "My God, my God, why have you forsaken me?" (Mt 27:46).

Like Jesus, Mary too had her culminating moment, her desolation, her forsakenness; she is the Desolate. When from the height of the cross, Jesus, indicating John, who represented all of us, said: "Woman, behold your son!" (Jn 19:26), those words sounded in her like a substitution. Mary underwent the trial of losing Jesus, not just because he was dying, but also because someone else was taking his place. And she accepted it. And with her new fiat at the foot of Calvary she let go of Jesus and thus became the mother of all, taking on the motherhood of countless human beings.

Mary Desolate is the Mother par excellence. In her desolation, in the peak of inexpressible sorrow and love, we have always seen God's plan for her completely fulfilled. There at the foot of the cross, Mary becomes mother not only of Jesus but of his Body which is the Church. She is the universal mother who holds together, with her love, all human beings, her children; she makes them brothers and sisters in the same way earthly mothers do. She is the mother of unity, the bond of unity for all her children.

And for this reason we have always linked all she represents to this aspect of love which is communication, indispensable for attaining unity, and have taken the Desolate as patroness of our means of communication. In the preceding conference, thinking of Mary, we noted how communicators inspired by the charism of unity know the qualities of a mother. And if Jesus Forsaken seemed to us to be the pupil of God's eye open onto the world, we can say that Mary Desolate seems to us a kind of *camera obscura,* taking in all that is negative in the world. But just as from a film negative we develop a positive image, she transforms situations in such a way that in what is negative, we can also see the positive. Mary is the type and figure of the Church, and so it is evident that in such a sublime creature all Christians can find a model for themselves; but I think professionals in communication can in a particular way find in Mary Desolate the model for their own perfection.

From the beginning Mary appeared to us in two guises: as a monument of virtue and as an icon of the gospel's most profound law: knowing how to lose. "For those who want to save their life will lose it, and those who lose their life for my sake will save it" (Lk 9:24).

Mary Desolate—Monument of Virtue

Mary at the foot of the cross, in her heart-rending *stabat* that makes of her a bitter sea of anguish, is the highest expression in a human creature of heroism in every virtue.

In her is the triumph of the virtues of faith and hope through the charity that enflamed her throughout her life, and here set her ablaze as she participated in such a living way in the Redemption.

The picture of her as mother who bears God dead in her arms yet still believes, hopes, and loves can be the model and support for communicators who, in order to transmit the news, often have to be present at events which in different ways call to mind the forsakenness of the Son of God crucified. Faith like that of the Desolate and a hope against all hope modeled on hers will allow them to avoid turning away from human tragedies and make them participate more with the greatest respect for the truth, but above all for persons. By being love themselves, as she was, they will be able to find the golden thread that runs through things and to unveil to many the more true and profound vision of reality, one capable of discerning the love of God beyond the complex pattern of human events.

Their word then will be like Mary's, who in the Magnificat saw into events more deeply and prophesied the wonders that God would work through his Son, while at the same time conquering with love injustice and abuse of power.

The Desolate is meekness par excellence, gentle, poor to the point of losing her Son who is God: all qualities absolutely vital for communicators who in a discreet but effective way can often facilitate dialogue and act as "mediators" through their way of reporting the news, as well as doing the same at the various sites to which their work calls them. Mary Desolate is the righteous one who does not complain when deprived of what was given her purely by election; the pure one in emotional detachment, tested to the utmost, from her Son who is God; the strong one who endured—and remained standing—while seeing Jesus die in the way he did. . . . Her example will help professionals in communication see events objectively and remain firm in service to the truth even when inconvenient and sometimes at personal cost.

Mary, in the desolation that clothed her with every virtue, furthermore will teach communicators to equip themselves with patience, perseverance, simplicity, and silence, so that in the night of what is human in them, there may shine out for the world the light of God dwelling within.

Always, in fact, the word must rest on silence, like a painting on a background. Silencing the creature in them and on this silence letting the Spirit of the Lord speak, professionals in communication will be more like Mary, the transparency of God. Then their word will not be merely word, but the Word with Silence! The Word with Being! It will be Love.

In this way communicators will acquire the prudence necessary to evaluate properly the situations about which they speak and verify the sources of their information. And even when they are a long time in the limelight, which can easily dazzle them, they will stay humble and know how to recognize the limits of their knowledge.

They will have the Wisdom indispensable for those who must comment on news events without distorting reality.

They will be capable of offering good counsel and have the gift of discernment to communicate only what deserves to be passed on, especially at a time like this when the flow of communication is intrusive and turbulent. The gospel presents Mary as the one who "treasured all these things in her heart" (Lk 2:51), yet no one ever spoke a word like her, who gave birth to the Word incarnate she later lost on Golgotha.

Mary Desolate, suspended in the void just like Jesus Forsaken, is in some way communication in its pure state, in which the communicator is only a *medium*, so much so as almost to disappear. This is transparency, that is, something which seems not to exist, but does. It is because it is not, like love. Is this not perhaps one of the greatest qualities of the *mediator*, the communicator? Does the media not find perfection when it forgets its own existence?

Icon of Knowing How to Lose

As I said, in our history Mary did not appear to us only as a monument of virtue, but also an icon of the most profound law of the gospel: she knew how to lose. Gospel love knows how to lose because it knows how to give. Precisely because she gives, she receives.

The Desolate lost, in order to do the will of God, that is, for God, even Jesus: her "Work." But precisely because she lost him, she found him again, many times over. In exchange for Jesus whom she gave it was impossible that she receive many partial Jesuses, but "other Jesuses" who are genuinely so, with his light and with his love. Just like him.

—Lubich, *Essential Writings*, 299–301

The Eucharist and the Transformation of the Cosmos

But the effect of the Eucharist in the human person goes further than that. For, as Saint Paul says: "The whole created world eagerly awaits the revelation of the sons of God.... The world itself will be freed from its slavery to corruption and share in the glorious freedom of the children of God" (Rom 8:19, 20). And this means that creation too is somehow called to glory.

Jesus who dies and rises again is certainly the real cause of the transformation of the cosmos. To accomplish the renewal of the cosmos, however, Jesus also expects the cooperation of people "Christified" by his Eucharist. In fact, Paul tells us that through our sufferings we complete "what is lacking in the sufferings of Christ" (see Col 1:24) and that nature "awaits the revelation of the sons of God" (Rom 8:19). One could say, therefore, that by means of the Eucharistic bread a person becomes "eucharist" for the universe, in the sense that joined with Christ he or she is the germ of the transfiguration of the universe.

Actually, if the Eucharist is the cause of the resurrection of the human person, is it not possible that the human body, divinized by the Eucharist, may be destined to decay under the ground in order to contribute to the renewal of the cosmos? We can say, therefore, that after we have died with Jesus we are the Eucharist for the earth. The earth eats us up as we eat the Eucharist, indeed not in order to transform us into earth but to transform the earth into "new heavens and a new earth" (Rev 21:1).

It is a fascinating thought that the bodies of Christians who have died have the task of collaborating with God in the transformation of the cosmos. This generates in our hearts deep affection and veneration for those who have preceded us. It gives us a better understanding of the age-old custom of venerating those whom we call the dead (especially saints' bodies) since they are really coming to a new life in the cosmos. The Eucharist redeems us and makes us God. We, after dying, cooperate with Christ in the transformation of nature, so that nature turns out to be like an extension of the body of Jesus. In fact Jesus, through the incarnation, took on human nature, which is where all of nature's elements meet.

—Lubich, *The Eucharist*, 53–54

3

SPIRITUALITY OF COMMUNION— LIVING JESUS WITHIN

Introduction

The next two chapters introduce the spirituality of communion of Chiara Lubich and the Focolare Movement. We have divided this approach to the spiritual life into two distinct but inseparable and intertwined aspects: "Living Jesus Within" and "Living Jesus in Relationships." The inner life with Jesus includes a special relationship with the "voice" of the Holy Spirit as well as a new way of life centered on the holiness within the Eucharistic communion as well as the holiness that promotes openness to dialogue outside of the Christian community. The chapter ends with a provocative and timely meditation on the four nights of the soul: the night of sense, the night of the spirit, the night of God, and the collective and cultural night.

Aspects for Ordering Daily Life and Activities

In this excerpt from Focolare: Living a Spirituality of Unity in the United States, *Thomas Masters and Amy Uelmen illustrate how the Focolare spirituality provides personal balance, citing* ninety-three-year-old Bessie's explanation of how she orders seven aspects of her daily life.

Speaking to young people, Chiara identifies a central human challenge: "We . . . easily slip into dividing and subdividing our life. We take one aspect of life, become passionate about it, and then this becomes our ideal: soccer, movies, art, science, philosophy, social problems. . . . We become specialists in our little idol, and for this reason we often have trouble understanding our neighbors."[1] In contrast, a person becomes fully human by letting God enter his or her life and "illuminate it in its entirety, like a sun placed in the center,"[2] a light that can penetrate and harmonize all of life's particular aspects.

A fulfilled life, then, comes not from maintaining "balance" but from discovering the integrity of the unifying presence of God in every specific aspect. "Like a ray of light that passes through a drop of water and opens out to display a rainbow," Chiara explains, "love, the life of Jesus in us, is manifested in different colors; it is expressed in various ways, each one different from the others."[3] For Focolare members, the "sun" of the life of God shines through every spiritual and practical aspect of their lives, from cooking, cleaning, working, and handling finances, to moments of prayer and liturgy, to how they approach illness and death. Nothing is more or less important, more or less sacred. The Focolare spirituality delineates seven aspects of life, each a way of expressing love:

---

1. Chiara Lubich, *Colloqui con i gen 1970–74* (Rome: Città Nuova, 1999), 18.
2. Lubich, *Colloqui*, 18.
3. Chiara Lubich, *A New Way: The Spirituality of Unity* (Hyde Park, NY: New City Press, 2006), 76.

- Work and sharing material and spiritual goods
- Outreach and witness
- Prayer and spirituality
- The natural world and health, both physical and spiritual
- Harmony and beauty of dress, home, and environment
- Wisdom and study
- Communication and media

The sense of integrity, "the wonderful unity" that comes as a result of living all these aspects together, permeates each person's entire existence. Chiara explains:

> Everything was to flow from love, be rooted in love; everything was to be an expression of the life of Jesus in us. And this would make human life attractive, fascinating. Consequently, our lives would not be dull and flat since they would not be made up of bits juxtaposed and disconnected.... No. Now it would always be Jesus who prayed, Jesus who engaged in mission, Jesus who worked, Jesus who ate, Jesus who rested, and so on. Everything would be an expression of him.[4]

Focolare members of every age and state of life strive to live this way. Bessie was ninety-three when she reflected on her approach. "It's not easy. Everything is just wearing out, and even the simplest tasks take a lot longer to get done." But she still aims to live all seven aspects:

---

4. Lubich, *A New Way*, 77.

1. Sharing Material Goods

I'm constantly eliminating things once thought to be indispensable. Recently, I gave something away that afterward I realized I still needed. Then I thought that the person would make good use of it, and God would take care of me. In fact, a few days later I received from someone else the same item I had given away. Giving as a lifestyle never ages, and the hundredfold (see Mt 19:29) is always new.

2. Outreach

Everyone understands the anxiety of children when they start school and have to make new friends, but no one thinks about how a ninety-year-old feels moving into an assisted-living facility. She too has to make new friends, and she can't even go home at the end of the day! I've had to learn to listen to people and figure out how each one wants to be loved.

3. Prayer

As I get older it actually gets easier to spend more time praying. I pray one rosary for my family, another for the Church and the Focolare family here and around the globe, and finally one for all of the problems in the world. I miss going to daily Mass and feel blessed whenever someone comes to take me, or the priest is able to come where I live. You might think that by ninety-three I would have worked out the kinks in my life, but I find myself making the same mistakes I've been trying to correct my entire life. Thank God I have learned how to start again.

4. Health

Even though it's clear that my holy journey is nearing its completion, it is still wonderful to be able to exercise, to eat properly, and to take all my medications. I have also been helped by John Paul II's "Letter to the Elderly" and by the example of his life. It takes a real act of faith to believe in the value of your life when many around you see things differently.

5. Harmony in Dress and Environment

I don't need many clothes or much furniture, but I try to keep what I have in order. With my eyesight so poor, I'm not sure if the colors match, and I might be tempted to think, "Who cares anyway?" But then I remember that even at ninety-three I have to try to express the beauty of God in the way I dress and the harmony of my apartment.

6. Wisdom and Studies

I've always loved learning new things, so I study the documents of the Holy Father and watch DVDs on the catechism or other topics. I'll never practice nursing again, but it is part of my vocation to stay on top of the latest advances in my profession. So I keep up to date because something I read or hear might be useful for someone else.

7. Communication

I used to send people cards or telephone them. Times have changed. I needed to learn to drive at fifty, and I now have had to learn how to use e-mail. Notwithstanding my eyesight, I watch the news every day, and I read every issue of *Living City* [the Focolare's bimonthly magazine] from cover to cover. Reading how the world tends toward unity helps me to be hopeful even in the midst of so much tragedy. I really believe in a united world. Focolare members learn about these seven aspects and help each other to live them in their daily lives. They are a frequent subject of discussion at periodic meetings, schools of formation, and conferences.

The aspects also serve as an organizing principle for Focolare gatherings, activities, and outreach events.

—Masters and Uelmen, *Focolare*, 43–45

Like a Rainbow

Chiara uses an analogy of the seven colors of the rainbow to explain the multifaceted aspects of the one life through the prism of the gift of love revealed in and through the triune God.

Through the charism of unity, the Lord wished to bring about in the Church not only a spirituality but also a society, which later was given the name Focolare Movement or Work of Mary.

Undoubtedly, this "Work" needs to have a soul (precisely what our communitarian spirituality is), but it also needs to have an order, a structure. And the Lord looked after this too.

If I remember correctly, it was in 1954. The spirituality appeared to be more or less complete. And one thing had become clear to us: we had to become another Jesus.

As early as 1946 we wrote in some notes: "Each of us must aim at being another Jesus as soon as possible. We must act as Jesus here on earth. We must put our human nature at God's disposal so that he can use it to make his beloved Son live again in us."[5]

But how could we do this? Baptism and the other sacraments had certainly already brought this about. But our adherence was necessary as well, and this could be summarized in one word: love. Love sums up the Christian law. If we love, we are another Jesus. And we are Jesus in all that

---

5. Chiara Lubich, "Unity" (December 2, 1946), quoted in *A Call to Love* (Hyde Park, NY: New City Press, 1989), 29.

we do. Our life, therefore, had to be love. If we had wanted to describe what we should be, we would have had to say, "We are love," just as God is love. And if love was our life, love had to be our rule as well.

And here is an idea we had, perhaps an illumination. Love is light; it is like a ray of light that passes through a drop of water and opens out to display a rainbow, whose seven colors we admire; they are all colors of light, which in turn display an infinite number of shades.

And just as the rainbow is red, orange, yellow, green, blue, indigo, and violet, love, the life of Jesus in us, is manifested in different colors; it is expressed in various ways, each one different from the others.

- Love, for example, leads to communion; it is communion. Jesus in us, because he is Love, brings about communion.
- Love is not closed within itself, but by its nature it spreads. Jesus in us, Love, reaches out to others in love. Love elevates the soul. Jesus in us raises our souls to God. This is union with God; this is prayer.
- Love heals. Jesus, Love in our hearts, is the health of our souls.
- Love gathers people together in assembly. Jesus in us, because he is Love, joins our hearts.
- Love is the source of wisdom. Jesus in us, Love, enlightens us.
- Love gathers many into one; this is unity. Jesus in us fuses us into one.

These are the seven main expressions of love we had to live, and they represent an infinite number of expressions.

These seven expressions of love immediately appeared to us as the standard for our personal life, and they would also constitute the Rule of the Work of Mary as a whole, and later on of its various branches.

Because love is the principle of each of the above expressions, of each aspect (since it is always Jesus who lives in us in every aspect of life), our life would be marked by a wonderful unity.

Everything was to flow from love, be rooted in love; everything was to be an expression of the life of Jesus in us. And this would make human life attractive, fascinating. Consequently, our lives would not be dull and flat since they would not be made up of bits juxtaposed and disconnected (with the time for lunch, for example, having nothing to do with the moment for prayer, and with mission set aside only for a specific hour, and so on).

No. Now it would always be Jesus who prayed, Jesus who engaged in mission, Jesus who worked, Jesus who ate, Jesus who rested, and so on. Everything would be an expression of him.

—Lubich, *A New Way*, 75–77

Becoming Saints as Church

How easy it is to notice a profound desire beginning to take hold in Christians; I would even call it an urgency. They show a desire to serve the Church not so much and not only in outward, material ways but in a different manner, more in tune with their faith, more essential.

One sees, especially among laity, that the way people used to think about becoming saints is not much appreciated; indeed, at times they consider it outdated. The style of sanctity for today's Christian goes beyond that of perfection sought individually, and they often express it like this:

we want to become saints together; we desire a collective sanctity.

So here and there we see committed Christians forming groups who, in unity, go toward God.

In fact it seems to us that this is what God really wants, so long as it all has the stamp of openness, the pulse of the entire Church, a loving unity with the hierarchy.

The face of the Church, with its lights and shadows, ought to be in every Christian, in every group of Christians. This means that we must feel as our own not only the Church's joys, her hopes, her constantly new forms of growth, her victories, but above all we must feel as our own all of her sorrows: the lack of full unity among the Churches, negative disputes, the threat of discarding age-old treasures, the anguish that many deny or refuse the message God speaks to the world for its salvation.

In all these afflictions, above all in the spiritual ones, the suffering Church appears as the Crucified Christ of today who cries out: "My God, my God, why have you forsaken me?"

Not long ago, I was at Mount La Verna. There I meditated on the exceptional gift of the stigmata that God gave Francis as a seal of his imitation of Christ, of his discipleship.

I was thinking that all true Christians should be stigmatics, not in an extraordinary, outward sense but spiritually.

I seemed to understand that the stigmata of today's Christians are the mysterious but real sufferings of the contemporary Church.

If the charity of Christ is not wide enough in us to feel in ourselves the pain of these wounds, we are not how God wants us to be today.

In these times, only an individual sanctity is not enough, nor one that is communitarian but closed. We must feel within ourselves the sorrow and also joy that Christ experiences today in his Bride.

We need to become saints as Church.

—Lubich, *Essential Writings*, 117

The Holy Spirit

Before [the experience of 1949], the Holy Spirit had worked in us to prepare our souls. The most important aspects of this preparation were the points of the spirituality which we had already begun to live. It was clear to us that we had to live God who is Love and that we had to respond to his love by doing his will. The will of God was then manifested in loving our neighbor and living the new commandment. We had already understood Jesus Forsaken and Jesus in the midst. So we were already living all these things.

The Extraordinary Effects of Living the Word

We had reached the point of understanding more about the Word of God, which we lived with great intensity, every minute, always. We weren't superficial about it. For example: "Love your neighbor as yourself" (Mt 22:39). All through the day we focused on loving our neighbor, our neighbor, all day long, with an intensity that was never again repeated.

The Word of God transformed us because, whereas before we might have thought of loving only our brother or sister, our family and friends, when we began to live the Word of God, we understood that we had to love everyone. As a result, our soul was revolutionized, our whole life became Gospel. . . . This "people of God born from the Gospel" began to grow.

Since the Word, every Word, had been pronounced by God, who is Love, we discovered in a totally new way that every Word contains love. How did we discover this? It was somewhat extraordinary . . . because each time we lived a Word of God, allowing it to enter our soul, it was transformed into fire, into flames. But we didn't understand. Then another Word entered. . . . Even though the Words of God are different from one another: "Love your neighbor." "Blessed are the pure of heart." Each time we lived any one of them, within us there was a fire—a spiritual fire, of course—a blaze.

A Special Relationship with the Holy Spirit and His "Voice"

I would like to tell you about our close relationship with the Holy Spirit up to that point, how we lived with the Holy Spirit in the years preceding 1949.

The first thing we understood about the Holy Spirit was when we told one another, prompted by the charism and not realizing what we were saying, "Listen to that voice!" [Someone would ask:] "How should I behave, what should I do?" [We answered:] "Listen to that voice," as if to say, "Your conscience will tell you; remember that in baptism we received the Holy Spirit, so listen to that voice."

In order to know how to go ahead on the right path, we always listened to that voice. Indeed, when we had Jesus in our midst, that voice became twice as clear, three times as clear. We understood God's will more clearly and were able to follow it.

In the First Place: God and His Will

What else does the Holy Spirit do within us? He helps us to choose the will of God, and he helps us to change our lives completely, because he makes us put everything else aside and choose God alone. He helps us to put God in the first place.

The Holy Spirit Binds Us Together in Unity through the Eucharist

Furthermore, the Holy Spirit is the one who makes us one heart, because he links us to one another. He is Love and he makes us one heart. He is the one who, from the beginning, urged us to go to Mass and receive the Eucharist. We weren't the ones who got the idea to receive communion every day. He was the one who told us, because he knew what the Eucharist brings about.

The Holy Spirit Guides Us toward Holiness and Blows Gently within the Christian Community

He changed us completely from within because he always led us to do our utmost. He guided us toward holiness by setting us on the path of our "Holy Journey." We had understood that the special atmosphere that is created—perhaps here in this moment, too—this special atmosphere of attention, which isn't always present, is the Holy Spirit. It's the gentle breeze of the Holy Spirit. He is the soul of the Church, of the Mystical Body of Christ.

—Lubich, *The Holy Spirit*, 24–27

Detachment

A reflection by Chiara on how true Christianity infuses every aspect of life

Gospel: St. Luke 14:26–33.[6]

> [Whoever comes to me and does not hate father and mother, wife and children, brothers and sisters, yes, and even life itself, cannot be my disciple. Whoever does not carry the cross and follow me cannot be my disciple. For which of you, intending to build a tower, does not first sit down and estimate the cost, to see whether he has enough to complete it? Otherwise, when he has laid a foundation and is not able to finish, all who see it will begin to ridicule him, saying, "This fellow began to build and was not able to finish." Or what king, going out to wage war against another king, will not sit down first and consider whether he is able with ten thousand to oppose the one who comes against him with twenty thousand? If he cannot, then, while the other is still far away, he sends a delegation and asks for the terms of peace. So therefore, none of you can become my disciple if you do not give up all your possessions.]

It is useless to fashion a Christianity and fool ourselves that we are building up Christ in us (meaning that we are his disciples, putting his Word into practice) if first we do not break our blood ties, displacing father, mother, brothers and sisters, children, and so on, from our heart, our mind, our strength, to place in our heart, mind, and so on, the Father, God, as he was for Jesus. And here we understand

---

6. This was the Gospel reading in the liturgy of that day, October 26, 1949 (editors' note).

his example in dealing with his Mother in this way:[7] when before her he gives place to whoever does God's will, when he tells her that he must do his Father's will.

So the one who belongs to Unity, and who thus can live Christ, is whoever, negating his or her own will, becomes empty to embrace any will of God at all. That will (and it is God himself) drawing souls near (either as mother, spouse, children, and so on, or—in virginity—as brothers or sisters in Christ) makes him or her love them *for God*, in supernatural fraternity, restoring Unity (once broken by sin) which is the Family where *ONE* is the Father, God, and *all* the others are brothers and sisters.[8]

And so before God the bonds of blood have no value. Such things, in any case, we have in common with the animals.

God is interested in the divine bond, the Holy Spirit, that makes us children of God and brothers and sisters of one another, the sole bond of fraternity; for us to have this bond we need to break the others that hinder: *to break*, that is to say, to burn them with the Holy Spirit, who is a consuming Fire. He, wishing to work a second birth in us (the birth that makes us children of God in perfect unity between the human being and grace, God given through participation), consumes all in himself, divinizing, setting all ablaze, translating all into Fire, into God, into true children of God as Jesus, in whom there was the hypostatic union, which we relive by being, we too, through participation, God-who-is-*human*, via hypostatic union (in some fashion),[9] ever more one, with the two natures ever *more distinct*.

---

7. In those moments, seeing in her simply his natural mother.

8. The universal dimension of love expressed here is typical of our charism, which is the charism of *Ut omnes*. Therefore these things that sounded new then, are so still now.

9. Anselm Stolz, having recalled that the human being justified by

* * * *

Therefore this total availability to God's will, whatever it might be, is the basis for building up Christians who from the very beginning (see the first commandment) must "*Love God* with *all* their heart, with *all* their soul, and so on."[10]

Therefore detachment from one's relatives is obligatory for the Christian. We should have no illusions, nor water down the Gospel. This is how it is. These are the disciples of Jesus, not just those who are consecrated.

And it is necessary also to let go of *life*, that is, one's own soul. Yes, *everything*.

And it is right. All is of God and we must love him *above everything*.

And it is beautiful, Jesus being so demanding, because he exposes himself as *God*. Only God can make demands like this. He is God and our brother who calls his brothers and sisters to follow him; he is the teacher who calls his disciples: a divine teacher, that is, a teacher-love because he first opens the road he makes others take.

He is truly God-Love! Love that adapts itself as a mother who makes herself *one* with her child.

What sadness to see his words not taken as they are and what need to re-preach *his Word*! And what joy because it is all a revolution: no one today is a true disciple of Christ: let us be so and make others be so too—*all: all one*.

And our personal cross as well must be taken up so as to be his disciples!

How much there is to do! And how antichrist are

---

the Holy Spirit (who forms in the person the image of the Son of God) is grafted into the Mystical Body of Christ, says that this union of the human being with the Son "can be described . . . as 'accidental-hypostatic'" (*La Scala del Paradiso: Teologia della mistica* [Brescia: Morcelliana, 1979], 131).

10. See Mt 22:37.

Christians,[11] truly and actively, wanting even to shed the cross that is the one thing that ought to be picked up, after having left everything, to be disciples of Jesus!

And Jesus tells us two parables.

The tower to be built:[12] recalling that life is a building up of Jesus in us.

And warfare:[13] recalling that to build Jesus it is necessary to fight with forces at least equal to those of the enemy, which is the world, the devil.

And our weapons are God in our heart in place of other things and the cross upon our shoulders. Beautiful, beautiful! The cross is a weapon because it is our source of Light:[14] it is the armor of God's children on earth.

God can be on earth, yes, in us but covered by the cross. We must be a living Jesus Forsaken.

Whoever builds a tower without calculating the cost will be laughed at. That is why the self-righteous types who display themselves as Christians because they make novenas and go to church are made fun of.[15] Rightly so: they are not Christians. They are dead masks, for God is not in them because they have no light, being stuffed with many things but not with him, and often they complain about the cross.

* * * *

---

11. In opposition to Christ's requirements.
12. See Lk 14:28–30.
13. See Lk 14:31–33.
14. Beyond the Wound, the Holy Spirit who gives light is acting in the soul.
15. Here is meant those who devote themselves solely to the minutiae and external practices of worship and not so much to taking up the cross or loving their brothers and sisters. They are made fun of because the world does not accept this kind of religiosity.

"So therefore, *whoever* of you does not renounce *all* they have cannot be my disciple."[16]

"Whoever": therefore the words of Jesus are addressed to all Christians.

"*All*": he demands it of everyone so as to be Christians. We cannot be attached even to our soul (which is one of our possessions); but we have to detach ourselves from everything. And here Jesus Forsaken is the universal Teacher.[17]

> —Unpublished document, *Paradise '49*, paragraphs 851–73. Used with permission of the Focolare Office for Wisdom and Study

You Are Everything; I Am Nothing

With one accord, saints, great saints, when touched by the grace of God, express a profound truth; nearly prostrate on the ground, as dust in the dust, they cry out to God, at first with their voices, but then with the immolation of the whole of their being: "You are everything; I am nothing."

While some see the footprints of God in creation and use nature as a stairway to the Creator, others take a different path. They fly without propellers, like a modern jet plane compared with the flying machines of the past. There, at the point where nature is extinguished, where creation makes itself nothing, they take flight, and making themselves nothing along with creation, sharing with love in that death, they sing the glory of God.

Just so. For a star shining in the heavens proclaims that God has made it, but a star being extinguished in the heavens announces its nothingness, reminding the saints who

---

16. See Lk 14:33.
17. What I say here at that time seemed extremely new compared to the Christian formation that we first focolarine had received as well.

know how to perceive the pleasing harmonies and silences of all things, through the silent Word living in them, that Another is the All, Another is light eternal.

And so at evening, a time of sadness for people, the setting sun gives rise in the hearts of the saints to a dawn, and the evening that falls is the voice that makes increase the eternal day that is God. And suffering, which gnaws the bodies of the saints or rends their souls, in the decomposition of the organic unity that is health and of the earthly tranquility that is peace, is taken by them as the voice of the One who is and who is Bliss.

If God is everything, to say that God is *everything*, it is necessary that mortal beings sing their own death, glorify him with their own nothingness. And this process, terrifying for most people, is intoxicating for saints because at the center of their lives is Life, which like a flame lit by the Lord can shed its light better when what surrounds it is reduced, as it must be reduced, to complete darkness.

Mary glorifies the Lord because she has made of her soul and her body a candle to be consumed to his glory.

And in God she found, though certainly she never sought it, her own glory, the greatest glory that earth knows after that of the Trinity.

—Lubich, *Essential Writings*, 154

The Attraction of Modern Times: A Poem by Chiara Lubich

This is the great attraction
of modern times:
to penetrate to the highest contemplation
while mingling with everyone,
one person alongside others.

I would say even more:
to lose oneself in the crowd
in order to fill it with the divine,
like a piece of bread dipped in wine.
I would say even more: made sharers in God's plans for humanity,
to embroider patterns of light on the crowd,
and at the same time to share with our neighbor
shame, hunger, troubles, brief joys.
Because the attraction
of our times, as of all times,
is the highest conceivable expression
of the human and the divine,
Jesus and Mary:
the Word of God, a carpenter's son;
the Seat of Wisdom, a mother at home.

—Lubich, *Essential Writings*, 169

A New Way of Life

And so here, at this point, I say: ours is a rather special spirituality; we must study it and see the differences between an individual and a collective spirituality.

First, I asked myself, have there been signs in our story that a collective spirituality was coming to life?

I remember the time, for example, when all of us, if we had died under the bombs, in the war, we wanted to be buried all together in one tomb, with the words written on it, "And we have believed in love." This "all together" gives the idea of a collectivity, not of an individual. It's not that I was thinking of being buried . . . it really was a question of being buried, because we could have died from one moment to the next.

Then another thing. Already at the start when we were in that cellar and read the last prayer of Jesus. Our whole spirituality came from there, which is really that of unity, unity among us and unity with God. That was another sign.

Other signs are found in the first letters I wrote to people about our great discovery of Jesus in the midst. I wrote: "But what is unity? It's hard to explain, you can't imagine it!" And I said beautiful things about this presence of Someone who was among us without our realizing it. I said: "It's Jesus." I said this but we didn't even realize it; but we were already living in that atmosphere.

Why is it that these individual spiritualities came to life, that after Pentecost many individual spiritualities grew up that no longer replicated that first descent of the Holy Spirit?

They came about because, at a certain point in the world, even around Christians, there was a lot of worldliness, so that the more fervent Christians withdrew from the world: It was the time of the hermits who withdrew and prayed in solitude. And they said some things we wouldn't understand. For example: "Flee from people, and you will be saved." Now we understand this in the sense that if someone harms you or wants you to do wrong, you have to flee—and fast! However, generally speaking, we remain in the midst of the world. So everything started back then, when people withdrew from the world and embraced another lifestyle.

Today, instead, the Holy Spirit calls us powerfully to go toward people, with people, together with people. This is the Holy Spirit. And our Movement did this too, twenty years before the Council, this going out toward people, without even realizing what we were doing.

Now, what is the difference between these spiritualities, that started with the hermits and onwards, and our spirituality?

Spirituality of Communion | 83

So, there are requirements for living these individual spiritualities, for example solitude, silence. They have a certain way of dressing, they want cloisters, cells, separation from the world, and so on. They also do many penances, fasting, harsh penances, and so on. That's another thing.

Then they take vows, but vows where what seems of most value is the vow itself, the ascetic part of the vow, that is, purity, poverty; they are all holy things but they've in some way been crystallized. Then they say many prayers; they pray a lot.

Now, what about us, what do we do instead? What are our requirements compared to what I listed as requirements for an individual spirituality?

Instead of solitude, we welcome our neighbors, we love company, we love unity with others. Instead of silence, we love the Word, and for everything, if just to give the Ideal. But speaking in everything: to share our gifts, to share what we've understood with others. Because Saint Lawrence Justinian says that the greatest glory you can give to God is to communicate what he's doing in you, the gifts within you; the greatest glory you can give to God. I don't know why this wasn't understood sooner.

And then we use words to talk about what we call the "instruments" of our collective holiness. To share what is in our souls we have to speak, to share about the Word of Life, we have to speak; to do the hour of truth we have to speak, to make the Pact itself, which is an act before God, you have to say it to someone: "I am ready to die for you." So, for us, the word is something sacred.

And, I repeat, we speak to give the Ideal. How can we evangelize without giving the Ideal? We always speak and use words. It's not that we reject silence, because if we need to be silent, like avoiding saying useless words, we have to be silent. If we are at Mass and we need to be silent, we love silence. It's not that we throw out all these things. I say that we *add* something—to silence we add the word, to solitude too. . . . Jesus says: "Go into your room to pray." So we go there sometimes, to be alone. Therefore, we don't reject solitude; we add that besides solitude, we welcome our neighbors. We add something.

Because as Father Castellano says, in our spirituality there's "something more." He says this "something more" is reciprocity and reaching unity, because you can love one another, but not reach unity, for example, which also presupposes unity of thought.

So there are all these things in our spirituality including the word.

We, in the world, know that we should not be *of* the world but remain in the world.

Considering our clothing, we dress like everyone else. Why? It's clear: because Jesus dressed like everyone else and Mary too. It's also because we don't want to seem too distant from the world or alienate people because of our clothes. We want to be close to them.

With regard to penances, yes, whatever we need to do that the Church asks us to do. If, for example, I don't know, it's necessary to fast on some days, we do it. It's not that we fail in this. For example, we deny ourselves with regard to certain TV programs or in front of certain worldly things or some inner impulses; all of this self-denial is absolutely necessary and we have to do them, these penances.

However, there is a characteristic penance of ours that is our neighbor, our neighbor. All the troubles that your neighbor brings you, you have to know how to overcome them and say: "This is my penance, it's my Jesus Forsaken. I have to embrace him and overcome it." So the typical penance of our collective spirituality is love of neighbor, who brings you, yes, heaven, if there is unity, but also purgatory, if there isn't unity.

Regarding prayers, we have our own prayers that we live very well . . . and here too, they are never only individual because we hear Mass for the whole world, for the Church. But there are those that are done more often on our own.

Now we have other practices that I am explaining a little at a time through our conference calls, the instruments of our collective spirituality, the Pact, sharing what's in our souls, sharing experiences of the Word, the moment of truth, and now all the others that will come too.

To sum it up, what is essential in a collective spirituality is having Jesus in the midst; and that he is always there. And if we do not have Jesus in the midst, we are like a monk outside his monastery, a monk who betrays his spirituality. He may be inside, but it's as if he were outside. Jesus in the midst is indispensable for us. He's indispensable at the beginning and indispensable at the end of the spiritual life, because we must build not only the "interior castle." That too, because we need union with God and God comes before everything else—but also the "exterior castle," that is, to put Jesus in the midst with everyone, in every group, in everything.

Because here we must always build so as to illuminate the whole Movement, our Work of Mary, and to bring this light to the Church, because now there are many bishops as you've understood, who live this Ideal and they're not inside the structures of the Movement; they're outside the structures. But when they live this Ideal among themselves and with the pope, they already have Jesus in the midst, and this is already the exterior castle that is the Church, not only the Movement.

Then, if they live this unity with people in their dioceses, and with the seven hundred bishops who are friends of the Movement, there will also be an exterior castle that is the Church and not only the Movement.

This is our dream. That is it.

> —Chiara Lubich to men and women Focolarini, "A Synthesis of the Collective Spirituality," Loppiano, Florence, November 29, 1994, in AGMF, ACL, Section 5. Unpublished document. Official translation by the Focolare Communication Office/Linguistic Services (COM-SL).

"A Spirituality for Dialogues"

In this talk from 1998, Chiara Lubich presents the foundations in the spirituality of communion for the Movement's engagement in multiple forms of dialogue.

What should be the key points, the essential cornerstones of what could rightly be called an *ecumenical spirituality*? Considering that the Church is a divine as well as a human reality, a first key point has to be God: and, given that this spirituality is a *spirituality of communion*, God as he is: Love (1 Jn 4:8). If we Christians, who are now at the dawn of the third millennium, take a fresh look at our two-thousand-year history, and in particular at the history of the second millennium, we cannot help but be saddened to see that it has often been marked by a series of conflicts, of quarrels, and of mutual incomprehension, which in many places have torn the seamless tunic of Christ that is his Church.

Who was to blame? Certainly, it came about by way of historical, cultural, political, geographical, and social circumstances. But it was also because among Christians there was a lack of what should be one of their specific unifying features: love. That is what happened.

And so today, as we seek to put right all that was wrong, and to find new strength to start again, we must focus our attention on the source of our common faith, the great revelation of God-Love.

In these times it is God-Love who, in a certain way, must reveal himself anew to the heart of each individual Christian, and to the Church that we compose. God-Love, above all, must once again reveal himself in each one of us . . . to each one of us, in the meantime.

How could we think of loving others with the fruit of reaching a fuller communion among Churches, if we ourselves don't feel profoundly loved, and if we Christians don't have in ourselves the certainty that God loves us?

The fact is that even though, through faith, we know that God is love, we don't often think of it, and we live as though we were alone on this earth, orphans, as though we did not have a Father caring for us in everything and through everything. A Father who counts even the hairs on our head, who knows all about us, and who wants to make everything work together for our good, whether the good we do or even our wrongdoing that he permits.

To set out to live an *ecumenical spirituality*, what is needed is that we make our own, with total conviction and honesty, the words of John the evangelist: ". . . We believe in love" (1 Jn 4:16). But God does not only love us as individual Christians, he loves us also as Church. And he loves the Church both for those times when throughout history it has acted according to the design that God had for it, but also, and here we see the wonder of God's mercy, for the times when, because Christians became divided from one another, it didn't correspond to his design, providing now they seek full communion again in the divine will.

It is this very consoling conviction which made Pope John Paul II, trusting in the One who brings good from evil, give the following answer when he was asked: "Why did the Holy Spirit permit all these divisions?" While recognizing that it could have been because of our sins, the Pope added: "Could it not be that these divisions have also been . . . a path continually leading the Church to discover the untold wealth contained in Christ's Gospel and in the redemption accomplished by Christ? Perhaps all this wealth [emerged in the different Churches—I add] would not have otherwise come to light."[18]

Therefore to believe in God, who is Love, for us and for the Church: this is the starting point. But, if God loves us, we cannot remain inactive before such divine goodness. As true children we must return his love and here too we must do so as individuals and as Church.

As individuals we do so by acting as Jesus did: he loved the Father, wanting the Father's will in the place of his own. Now, the divine will is written above all in Holy Scripture, especially in the New Testament for us.

It is a duty for those who want to commit themselves to unity, and therefore it is a key point of a possible *ecumenical spirituality*, to live out the words of the Gospel, one by one.

Cardinal Bea said that the more Christians live the Word, the more it makes them similar to Jesus and thus more similar and united to one another.

Christians should make all the words of Sacred Scripture their own; in particular the words which sum up the Law and the prophets: love of neighbor (see Mt 22:40). Only

---

18. Pope John Paul II, *Crossing the Threshold of Hope* (New York: Knopf, 1995), 167.

the person who loves others with the same charity as God's will be an authentic Christian today. And here I would like to pause. We will never repeat it enough: Gospel love, which we owe our neighbor, is a special love. It has its own unique qualities: for example, it aims to see Christ in every neighbor. At our final judgment, he will count as done to Him what good or evil we have done to others.

This charity must go out toward all people. Christians do not distinguish between those who are beautiful or ugly, nice or difficult, white or black, compatriot or foreigner, American or African, Christian or Buddhist, and so forth. They love everyone. This charity always takes the initiative; Jesus loved us first when we were still sinners. We should not expect to feel loved; we have to love everyone, by taking the initiative.

It is a charity that makes us love each person as ourselves, that makes us one with brothers and sisters: in sufferings and in joys.

And the Churches too should love with this same love.

Jesus prayed, "Father, may they all be one" (see Jn 17:21). But instead we appear always ready to forget his testament, and to scandalize the world with our divisions, the world we should be winning over for him.

Over the centuries each Church has, to a degree, become set in its ways, because of the waves of indifference, lack of understanding, and even of mutual hatred. What is needed in each Church is a supplement of love; or rather Christianity needs to be invaded by a torrent of love.

So we need love and mutual love between Christians, and mutual love between the Churches. The love that leads people to put everything in common, each Church to be a gift for the others, so that we can foresee in the Church of the future that there will be just one truth, expressed in different ways, seen from different viewpoints, made more beautiful by the variety of interpretations.

In his book *Crossing the Threshold of Hope*, Pope John Paul II writes: "It is necessary for humanity to achieve unity through plurality, to learn how to come together in the one Church, even while presenting a plurality of ways of thinking and acting, of cultures and civilizations."[19]

It is not that one Church or another will have to "die" (as is sometimes feared), but each Church should be reborn as new in unity. Living in this Church in full communion will be something marvelous, as fascinating as a miracle, which will attract the attention and interest of the whole world.

Mutual love, however, is truly evangelical, and therefore valid, only if it is practiced in the measure wanted by Jesus: He said: "Love one another as I have loved you. There is no greater love than this, that a man should lay down his life for his friends" (see Jn 15:12–13).

But how did Jesus give his life? In his passion, Jesus did not only suffer during the agony in the garden, when he was scourged, crowned with thorns, and when he was crucified, but he also suffered in that climax of suffering which he expressed in the cry: "My God, my God, why have you forsaken me?" (Mt 27:46). It was a suffering which, as theologians and mystics affirm, was his greatest trial, his darkest night. Now, in order to reach the goal of building full communion in mutual love, it seems necessary today to reflect on and to mirror our lives especially in that suffering. It is understandable. If Jesus was called to overcome the sin of the world and, therefore, the division of people cut off from God and, as a result, divided among themselves, he could only fulfill his mission by experienc-

---

19. John Paul II, *Crossing the Threshold of Hope*, 167.

ing in himself the extreme depths of separation: the separation of him, God from God, by feeling he was forsaken by the Father.

But Jesus, by re-abandoning himself to the Father ("Into your hands I commend my spirit" [Lk 23:46]) overcame that immense suffering and brought people once more into the bosom of the Father and in mutual embrace. But if this is so, it is not difficult to see in Him, in Jesus Forsaken, the brightest star that can shed light on our ecumenical journey. He is the pearl that we need to discover in order to bear great fruit. An *ecumenical spirituality* will be fruitful insofar as those who dedicate themselves to it see in Jesus crucified and forsaken, who re-abandons himself to the Father, the key to understanding every disunity and to re-establishing unity. For a productive ecumenism we need hearts touched by Him, who love Him, choose Him, and who know how to see his divine image in every disunity they encounter, and who find in Him the light and the strength not to get stuck in the traumas and in the cracks of division, but to always go beyond and find a solution, all possible solutions.

Mutual love leads then to achieving unity.

When unity is lived it has an effect, which is also, so to say, a key point for a vibrant ecumenism. We are speaking about the presence of Jesus among people gathered in his name. He said, "For where two or three are gathered in my name, I am there among them" (Mt 18:20). And this is already a strong bond between us and helps us on the journey toward visible unity! Jesus present between a Catholic and a Waldensian who love one another, between Anglicans and Orthodox, between an Evangelical-Lutheran and a Methodist. . . . This presence of Jesus is a gift which also lessens the pain of waiting for the day when we will all share together his presence in the Eucharist.

And another key point of an *ecumenical spirituality* must be a great love for the Holy Spirit. This year we must make an effort to better know the Holy Spirit, Love Personified, who binds in unity the Persons of the Blessed Trinity and is the bond between the members of the Mystical Body of Christ.

Then, we must not forget Mary, who was proclaimed by the Council of Ephesus, a Council we share, as Mother of God, Theotokos. A mother always helps her children to come together.

And we need to love the Church as communion and, especially for us Catholic Christians, to love the Holy Father whose Petrine ministry serves the unity of the Church and, with it, to love the Church hierarchy.

An *ecumenical spirituality* lived in this way can produce exceptional fruits.

But we can foresee that it will have one effect above all. Since it is communitarian, it will bind into one all those who live it, so that there will be solidarity among them and they will be, in a certain way, already one. They will realize that they form, so to speak, one Christian people, and that together with all that is being done in so many other ways through the action of the Holy Spirit in this ecumenical age, they can be a leaven helping to bring full communion among Churches. In fact, it will be the living out of a fourth ecumenical dialogue, in addition to the dialogues of charity and of prayer and the theological one. It will be the *dialogue of the people*. Not a people formed only of laity, of course, but the whole people of God.

It is a dialogue which will enable us to discover more clearly, and more effectively, the rich heritage already shared by Christians, including Baptism, Sacred Scripture, the first Councils, the Fathers of the Church, etc. This dialogue will enable us to give greater value to this heritage and to live it together.

We are eager to see this people, and already here and there it can be glimpsed, and we long to see it in every Church.

As you can readily understand, a *spirituality of communion* not only helps bring unity among Christians but also opens up dialogue with people of other religions. This dialogue is one of the most demanding and urgent challenges we face at the dawn of the third millennium.

And here, first of all, we wish to remember Judaism and the Jewish people, to whom—as we mentioned—today the Catholic Church in Italy is dedicating a special day of reflection entitled: "What is humankind that you are mindful of them, human beings that you care for them" (see Ps 8:5), which has as its theme the unique and essential role of the human being in their tradition.

The biblical proclamation that the human person is made in the image of God is not found in any other religious traditions except for Judaism and Christianity, and this implies the supreme and intangible dignity of the human person. Therefore, we find in the Judaic tradition the roots of what today are defined as "human rights." What should we say about these brothers and sisters of ours that John Paul II called our "elder brothers and sisters"?

We Christians will never wholly understand what it means to share with them our common faith in the one God of Abraham. If we travel the road of a deeper reconciliation with them, we will then be able to glorify God together, to thank Him, ask Him forgiveness, "side by side" (Zeph 3:9), all together as His creation, as His children and therefore, as brothers and sisters among us.

Together with them, we can allow ourselves to be enlightened and nourished by the heavenly treasures we hold in common, contained in the Jewish Bible, almost identical to our Old Testament. We can have great hope for the good of humanity, because of our deep fraternal communion with them. Together with them, we can double our witness of God the Creator of the universe to the whole world. But we need to get to know each other better, to work together and even live moments of prayer in common—such as today—to render real and visible a profound unity of spirit that exists notwithstanding all our differences and our wounds of the past, which often Christians were guilty of inflicting.

In recognizing the other person as a brother or sister in his or her diversity, we can become always more aware of the fact that even the roots of our specific Christian faith are found in this people, because Jesus was Jewish, Mary was Jewish, Peter and Paul and the other first apostles were Jewish.

This same Abrahamic faith also links us with the Muslims—even though with them the relationship is very different. We too have wonderful experiences of deep and fruitful dialogue with them.

In addition, if we Christians love as this spirituality teaches us, we will have an ulterior light to see and discover in other faiths the presence of the "seeds of the Word," as the Council calls them.[20] The non-Christian faiths, in fact, "often reflect a ray of that Truth that enlightens all men and women."[21] And this discovery can foster closeness and mutual understanding. And as it is true that almost all religions have the so-called "Golden Rule," which in different

---

20. See Vatican II, *Ad gentes* 11: "Semina verbi in eis latentia."
21. See Vatican II, *Nostra aetate* 2: The non-Christian faiths "often reflect a ray of that Truth which enlightens all men and women."

ways, says: "Do to others what you would wish done to you; do not do to others what you would not want done to you," it will be possible to establish with them, on the basis of this Rule, a relationship of mutual love.

Then there is the dialogue with those who have non-religious convictions, based on a common esteem for true values such as peace, freedom, life, human rights, ecology, and so forth.

And there is the dialogue between peoples. And unity between the human person and nature.

A *spirituality of communion*, then, and unity as the keynote that can sum it all up, which is certainly not uniformity. If we put unity into practice we will see the world change direction, like a film turning back to the beginning. There are so many traumatic divisions, so many crises, so much disintegration on our planet, which remain immersed in indifference, in secularization and materialism. With this new life we can turn back, while still going forward. Humanity will rediscover the unity God had in mind when he created it. This is my wish for you today, above all for those of us who would love to commit to living this spirituality of reconciliation and dialogue.

—Chiara Lubich on the Day of Reflection on Judaism, "A Spirituality for Dialogues," Cathedral of Palermo, January 17, 1998, published in *Città Nuova* (Rome), "Our Jewish Roots," 42, no. 3 (1998): 33. Official translation by the Focolare Communication Office/Linguistic Services (COM-SL)

The Four Nights

One of Chiara's great innovations was to think about the spiritual life as four nights. Specifically, she refers to the night of senses, the soul, God, and culture. In these excerpts from a talk given in Budapest, she explains the meaning of these four nights.

Many people realize that our lifestyle has a mystical dimension. I would actually say that it is a mystical way. This is manifested in various ways, depending on whether we are considering the night of the senses, or of the spirit, or the night of God.

Our spirituality clarifies the fact that the true Jesus Forsaken, whom we love, is very much joined to the sentence, "Father, into your hands I commend my spirit" (Lk 23:46).

Jesus Forsaken and the Risen Jesus are totally one with the realities of asceticism and mysticism. Here it is necessary to note that Jesus in his abandonment asked a question that requires an answer: the resurrection.

In fact, in suffering we see the ascetical effort, and in the light that comes from embracing it, the mystical aspect.

Living our ideal, in whatever kind of "night "we experience, we are always in this double state of soul, and what makes this possible is our relationship with Jesus Forsaken. He is the Master of both the ascetic aspect and the mystical aspect.

* * * *

They are called "nights" because that's what they are like.

The first night involves, in general, our senses, our humanity. You may experience a long illness, or the loss of loved one, or undergo big failures, like economic collapse, and so on.

The second night is the night of the spirit, which was

experienced, for the most part, by all the saints who were mystics.

In the following section, I have availed myself of definitions from the very valuable *Dictionary of Mysticism*, since it is a renowned publication.

It states that a "night" is "a prolonged and profound spiritual experience, characterized by the sensation of aridity, obscurity and emptiness, lived and accepted as the absence of God."

In the night of the spirit, the person experiences a "total loss of any support 'like someone hanging in the air with nothing to lean on,' without present, past or future."

Then another aspect of it is even more painful.

In the night of the spirit "the person doesn't only 'feel' aridity, darkness, torment, or misery, sin, impotence, but also 'believes' and interprets this as God being angry with them, punishing and abandoning them with reason. The person 'believes that they are so full of evil that they merit to be abhorred by God and for good reason banished forever by God.'"[22]

"This terrible burden and interior emptiness originates from, and is often accompanied by, distressing external circumstances, like tribulations, darkness, failures, persecutions, temptations."

"That which the person feels to be abandonment and even punishment is, in reality, a clear gesture of divine love and power. 'God teaches the soul and instructs it in the perfection of love, without the soul doing anything nor understanding how this is coming about.'"

"God illuminates and purifies the soul in a passive way

---

22. Luigi Borriello, E. Caruana, M. R. del Genio, and N. Suffi, eds., *Dizionario di Mistica* [Dictionary of Mysticism] (Vatican City: Libreria Editrice Vaticana, 1998).

through 'infused contemplation,' divine light that enlightens and dazzles, irritates the soul because of its immense bright light and because of the fragility of the soul. It makes the soul live and act with new motives and criteria that it does not comprehend."[23]

What is the difference between the night of the senses and the night of the spirit, and ourselves? The difference between a movement with a collective spirituality and a movement with a more individualistic spirituality is that the first begins the journey together with friends while the second involves people who go to God alone.

We begin not by ourselves, but together with others. We journey ahead together with others. We scale the mountain toward God with Jesus in our midst. We are already in Christ. So we walk along the ridge of the mountain because Jesus in our midst can only be on the top. And that's why we go along the ridge. We don't climb up a path, but instead reach the top of the mountain immediately.

The trials are the same as all the others have, but we have the advantage (and also the disadvantage) of journeying together. If the trials are sometimes softened, it's because they are lived with the help of Jesus in the midst, of Jesus in us and Jesus in our brother or sister.

* * * *

But there is a third night that is typically ours. It is the night of God.

On April 3, 1950, I wrote: "St. John of the Cross, who is the master of nothingness, teaches us that everything has to be annihilated in us so that God can enter. That is the meaning of his night of the senses and of the spirit."

---

23. *Dizionario di Mistica.*

God asks something more of us: he silences the senses, the intellect, the will, the memory, and even the inspirations of God.

Our life then is Jesus Forsaken. You live, like him, perfectly annihilated.

And this happens not only when many people come together and only one speaks. It happens always. When we speak with a brother or sister, we extinguish everything, even divine inspirations, in order to enter perfectly into that person, making ourselves nothing and, therefore, simple. Only what is simple can enter everywhere. And that's what it means to be one. And thus we can see that being one is being Jesus Forsaken.

* * * *

John Paul II did not hesitate to draw a parallel between the "dark night" of St. John of the Cross and the darkness of our times, which represents a sort of collective "night" into which humanity continues to fall, especially in the West.

It's clear to everyone that we need strong ideas, an ideal that opens a way that can give an answer to the numerous anguished questions of our day, a light to be followed, all the way to the point of saying with St. Laurence, "My night has no darkness, but all things break forth in light."[24]

In his apostolic letter *Novo millennio ineunte*, John Paul II announced a new star on our journey: Jesus Crucified and Forsaken. He said, "We shall never exhaust the depths of this mystery. . . . 'My God, my God, why have you forsaken me?'" (Mk 15:34).[25]

---

24. See https://www.newmanreader.org/works/times/tract75/section5.html.

25. *Novo millennio ineunte*, https://www.vatican.va/content/john-paul-ii/en/apost_letters/2001/documents/hf_jp-ii_apl_20010106_novo-millennio-ineunte.html, §25.

Jesus Forsaken is presented, therefore, to the whole Church, at the suggestion of John Paul II, but he is not the only one to do so. Some of the saints of centuries ago and a few modern theologians had already offered him to Christianity. And then there is our movement, in which Jesus Forsaken is central.

This is exactly what we want to propose today: Jesus who cried out, "My God, my God, why have you forsaken me?"

It was his inner passion, his darkest night, the peak and culmination of his suffering. It is the drama of God who cries out, "My God, my God, why have you forsaken me?"

It is an infinite mystery, an unfathomable suffering that Jesus experienced as man, and that shows the measure of his love for humanity, since he wanted to take upon himself the separation that kept us far from the Father and from one another. He took it upon himself and filled it to the brim.

Isn't he like a person who is in anguish, or alone, or spiritually dry, or disappointed, or a failure, or weak? Isn't he the image of every painful separation among brothers and sisters, among Churches, among large sections of humanity with contrasting ideologies? Isn't Jesus, who lost, so to say, the sense of God, who became "sin" for us (as Paul says), the symbol of the world that is against God, against the Church, plunged into every kind of abnormality?

Loving Jesus Forsaken we find the motivation and the strength to never flee from these evils, these divisions, but to accept them, consume them and give them our individual and collective remedy.

If we manage to meet him in every suffering, if we love him and repeat with Jesus on the cross, "Father, into your hands I commend my spirit" (Lk 23:46), the night will pass and we will find the light.

****

There is a second night of God that involves a total darkening of the soul. This is the trial that one lives at a certain point in life.

A new understanding of God opens up on a totally different level. It consists not only of the cry of Jesus Forsaken but also of every possible suffering, in particular in the spiritual realm. It is different from the night of the spirit, in which you at least feel that God is present and he is the one making you suffer.

You realize that this is another kind of night: the final "night" that one can experience here on earth.

What does it mean?

It means that God is extremely distant.

The soul feels alone, tormented by incredible sufferings. "To whom can I turn? Who can I lean on?" And yet in a particular way, one no longer feels God, in the sense that God has gone far away. He, too, goes out toward the far "horizon of the sea." We had followed him up to that point, but at the far edge of the sea, he disappears beyond the horizon, and one can no longer see him at all. At least this is how the person feels.

Therefore, while we had believed previously that the nights of the spirit ended by embracing Jesus Forsaken, we realize that in this instance we enter into Jesus Forsaken.

In his cry, Jesus in a certain way reproached the Father. In this kind of trial, the soul, in its immense sadness, is tempted to blame God.

One really has to speak of "beyond the horizon," where God is no longer visible and the soul descends so far down into this night that it loses everything for months and months, everything, truly everything.

It's a terrible shock: God is no longer felt. While up to the edge of the horizon, one could feel the pain, at this point, the person no longer feels God.

The soul is left alone.

The person is given the opportunity to understand up to what point God wants the soul stripped. One no longer believes, no longer loves, no longer remembers. One does not exist.

And the soul cries out, but faith does nothing for it. It asks for graces, but they are no longer there.

It truly does not exist. This is unbearable. . . . It is a participation in being "Jesus Forsaken-similar to hell." In other words, God abandons you.

You think: "God does not think about me, God does not remember me." Why? Why? Almost as if the Father had made a mistake by abandoning you.

Some months later, Chiara wrote:

"In those days, thinking of the grain of wheat that is destined to die, I felt dead in the 'abandonment—hell.' I could not imagine that any fruits could come from this.

"Now instead, from what we can see, the fruits are beyond anything that we could have imagined."

—Excerpts from Chiara Lubich, "Our Response to Today's Collective and Cultural Night," Budapest, September 16, 2006, in AGMF, ACL, Section 5. Unpublished document. Official translation by the Focolare Communication Office/ Linguistic Services (COM-SL)

4

SPIRITUALITY OF COMMUNION—
LIVING JESUS IN RELATIONSHIPS

Introduction

Dialogue is the chief charism of the Focolare Movement—within the Catholic Church, among Christians, with non-Christian religions, with those who profess no belief, and with "the spirituality that inundates the world." In these selections we see the centrality of a spirituality of dialogue, the diversity of the forms of dialogue, and the practical and spiritual challenges that arise in each of these contexts.

Sometimes dialogue is needed even within the same person, if that person is trained or instructed by more than one form of learning. The dialogue between science and religion is a good example of such an internal divide. As a result, of particular interest to the editors were the dialogues that have taken place with and from within the different disciplines of learning to which Chiara Lubich has made a contribution. We have included a few of the speeches given in the conferral of her many honorary doctorates to display her integrative and fruitful practical wisdom with respect to these divides in the academy, in our students, and beyond. The Abba School, with which this section ends, is a practical model for overcoming these divisions that has already been applied in multiple contexts.

The Four Dialogues

In the two excerpts that begin this chapter, we see Chiara Lubich's vision for the spirituality of unity as the soul of dialogue.

In her address to the "Convention for the Unity of Peoples," she describes the first dialogue as "within the Catholic Church." This dialogue also includes members of the Focolare who live the spirituality fully while professing their faith in other Christian churches. The second, "ecumenical dialogue," is a "dialogue of the people," a lived experience that demonstrates what the "Church that will come" will be. The third, "with people of other religions," is based on the common denominator among all the major faith groups—the golden rule. The fourth dialogue, among those who "do not profess any religious faith," is based on what she perceives as the DNA of love inscribed in their souls.

The Focolare Movement also engages in a fifth dialogue, in which the spirituality (and here she uses St. John Chrysostom's reference to the effects of the Holy Spirit) inundates the world. One of Lubich's close collaborators, Vera Araujo, describes an encounter with her in which she explains this "fifth dialogue" and its significance to the Focolare Movement.

From an Address to the Convention for the Unity of Peoples

The Focolare Movement has been involved in four dialogues for almost half a century.

The dialogue within the Catholic Church, which helps it to grow in "communion," that communion which ensures brotherhood and peace.

The ecumenical dialogue in its form of "dialogue of the people"—this is ours. This dialogue actively involves, in our Movement alone, Christians of 350 Churches, transforming everyone into one "Christian family," almost mirroring the soul of that one Church that will come.

The dialogue with people of other religions: Muslims, Jews, Buddhists, Hindus, Sikhs, etc., who are present today also in Europe due to widespread migration. This dialogue is possible because of the so-called "golden rule" common to all the major religions of the world. It says: "Do to others as you would have them do to you" (Lk 6:31). Ultimately, the golden rule asks that we respect and love every neighbor, so that if we love, because we are Christians, and if they love too, as Hindus, Muslims, and Jews, there is reciprocal love, from which brotherhood blossoms.

This dialogue has already brought about, through the Focolare Movement alone, a strong and sincere brotherhood with a modern Buddhist Movement of Tokyo, which numbers six million members. Also with an African American Muslim Movement which has two million members. Through the exchange of gifts in dialogue, this African American Movement opened to us in the United States forty mosques, where we can announce our experiences of faith, which they are always eager to hear, while we, on our part, open our little towns in continuing friendship.

Finally, dialogue with brothers and sisters who do not profess any religious faith—perhaps the majority—but who also have the impetus to love inscribed in the DNA of their soul.

How can we explain positive results, which offer great hope, in a single Movement?

The secret of its success lies in a new line of action, assumed by millions of people who, inspired basically by Christian principles—without neglecting but, on the contrary, highlighting parallel values present in other faiths and cultures—seek to bring brotherhood, peace, and unity into the world. It is the "spirituality of unity," both a personal and communitarian spirituality, timely and modern, which the Holy Father John Paul II has presented today under the name of "spirituality of communion" to all the Church so that everyone may live it.

This spirituality has two main foundation stones. The first was given to the initial group of young women while they sought refuge in a cellar from the bombings of World War II. They opened the Gospel at random to Jesus's solemn prayer to the Father shortly before his death: "Father . . . may they all be one" (see Jn 17:11–21). This prayer asks for the unity of Christians with God and with one another, to be extended then to everyone in a universal brotherhood.

The second foundation stone, Jesus crucified and forsaken, became clear to these young women when they learned more about the cry of Christ on the cross: "My God, my God, why have you forsaken me?" (Mt 27:46 and Mk 15:34). They had understood, in fact, that Jesus, the Word of God become man, precisely because he had become one of us, took upon himself all of our faults, divisions, and sufferings; this is why the Father permitted that he feel this very painful abandonment.

However, with an act of the will that was beyond human strength, he overcame this tremendous trial and re-abandoned himself to the Father saying: "Into your hands I commend my spirit" (Lk 23:46).

Therefore, Jesus who is forsaken, but who is also risen to become Love, has always been for the members of the Movement—and now, for others as well—the model, the key for recomposing every type of disunity, for healing every trauma.

By loving him, we have cooperated toward uniting individuals and segments of society in every nation, thus working toward the unity of the human family.

> —Chiara Lubich to participants at the Congress "Peace, Solidarity and Brotherhood: A Different Cooperation for the Unity of Peoples," Rimini, Italy, June 22, 2002, in AGMF, ACL, Section 5. Unpublished document. Official translation by the Focolare Communication Office/Linguistic Services (COM-SL)

Vera Araujo on the "Fifth Dialogue"
The first thing I would like to tell you is that it is always a joy for me to speak with you, above all to this branch of the Work of Mary, about the Inundations, also called the "Fifth Dialogue," which is developing and growing. It is interesting to be able to explain how this reality was born and is still growing, having behind it a strong thrust from Chiara. She has this reality in her hand, she looks at it from all sides and she drives it forward. If she gives directives, they are precise and precious guidelines.

To give you an idea of how strong Chiara's thrust is, I'll share with you the last piece of news I heard when . . . she said: *"The Inundations! I believe that these Inundations will have a great future, more than everything else, more than New Humanity, more than the Focolarini, because it is the Ideal dressed up as a human being. . . . In the Inundations we have the divine aspect, which is the Ideal, but incarnate . . . therefore they will have a great future. There will be a great future. . . . In my opinion they are the most beautiful part, because everyone is working to get there."*

What did she mean with these words, which poured out of her so spontaneously?

She meant to say that in the Inundations she saw God's project for the world, the relationship of the Ideal with the world and therefore the fitting channels to bring the Ideal into the world. As if to say: the Inundations are the structures inspired by God to reach all the possibilities we can have. And this makes us understand Chiara's expectations, the thrust she puts into it, how she takes care of this reality, how she keeps with it.

This gives us something of the context in which each Inundation is developing. Little by little, each one is finding its path, its road, its distinct evolution, each one different from the other.

This is very beautiful because we can see God's imagination, because to actualize an Inundation in the field of mass media, for instance, is not the same thing as to actualize it in the field of politics or in the field of psychology. They are cultural worlds which are very different, where each one has to find its own way, its own points of reference.

> —Vera Araujo to leaders of the Volunteers of God, Castel Gandolfo (Italy), January 10, 2002. Unpublished transcript of videotape. Used with permission of the Segreteria Centro Volontarie.

Chiara Lubich: "I Have a Dream for the New Millennium"

Wednesday, December 1, 1999
I dream that the atmosphere of our Church will be more suited to her as the Bride of Christ; a Church which shows

herself to the world as being more beautiful, more one, more holy, more charismatic, more in conformity with her model, Mary, therefore, Marian, more dynamic, more like a family, more intimate, more similar to Christ her Spouse. I dream of her as being a beacon for humanity. And I dream of seeing in her a sanctity of the people, as never before.

I dream that brotherhood, which is gaining momentum today in the consciences of millions of people, will be lived out more and more widely across the globe, so as to become in the future, in the next millennium, a general, universal reality.

Consequently, I dream of the relenting of wars, conflicts, hunger, and the thousand other evils in the world.

I dream of a more intense dialogue of love among the Churches so as to see in the near future the coming together of the one Church.

I dream of a more living and active dialogue among people of the most varied religions linked to one another by love, "the golden rule" present in all their sacred books.

I dream that the various cultures in the world will mutually enrich each other and draw closer to one another so that they may give origin to a world culture that highlights those values which have always been the true wealth of individual peoples, and I dream that these values will stand out as global wisdom.

I dream that the Holy Spirit will continue to inundate the Churches and potentiate the "seeds of the Word" beyond themselves, so that the world may be invaded by continual innovations of the light, life, and works which he alone is able to kindle. So that ever-greater numbers of men and women may set out toward straight paths, converge toward their Creator, and put their heart and soul at his disposal.

I dream of gospel-based relationships not only among

individuals, but also among groups, movements, religious and lay associations; among peoples, among States, so that it becomes logical to love the other's country as one's own. Likewise, that it becomes logical to tend toward a universal communion of goods, at least as the point of arrival.

I dream of a world united in the variety of peoples.

In a word, I dream of an anticipation of the new heavens and new earth as far as this is possible here on earth. I dream many things, but we have a millennium to see them come true.

—Chiara Lubich (ed. Zanzucchi), *Attualità*

The Charism of Unity and Philosophy

An Address upon Conferral of an Honorary
Doctorate Degree in Philosophy
(Jean-Baptiste de La Salle University,
Mexico City, June 6, 1997)

There is also a new philosophy that emerges from the life of the charism of unity.

Philosophy sometimes is called the science of the question "why" in the sense that it seeks to explore in depth whatever men and women ask about and, as much as possible, to give an answer. After years of intense spiritual life, living this new spirituality, we realized that there is a moment in Jesus's life that is pregnant with answers to all our "whys."

It is the moment before he dies, when Jesus addresses his immense "why" to the Father and unleashes that mysterious cry: "My God, my God, why have you forsaken me?"

Initially, however, when we decided to follow him in this way, we did not feel prompted so much to meditate on or to formulate the doctrine that may lie beneath his being forsaken. Instead, we immediately discovered his forsakenness as the key to recomposing every unity. It was placing Jesus Forsaken as the ideal of our life that gave us the courage to run wherever he was most present, and, by loving him, by consuming him in ourselves, we worked to relieve sufferings and to build unity. But Jesus Forsaken did not present himself to us only as the answer to the existential questions of humanity.

He is God who asks God "why," who asks the reason for a severed relationship that seems to touch the very unity of God! He is certainly the question, so to speak, carried to its deepest, most radical expression, where no human question dares to go. Thus, he seems to be the one who best represents human intelligence in the face of mystery. At the same time, he cries out his great "why" precisely in order to give us the answer to the many "whys" which are more properly the object of philosophical reflection, as the Abba School seeks to point out.

I will give two examples of this reflection, briefly and simply.

Let us consider the first: the mystery of being.

What answer does he give us?

Though there may be a number of ways of defining it according to various cultures, in essence, the fundamental affirmation of human thought is: being is. It is the acknowledgment of that great ocean of existence in which human beings are immersed in communion with everyone and everything. This is the simplest, single, and primordial certainty from which we can then begin to penetrate the multiple and complex layers of reality. Everything can be negated, except being.

We find being in whatever is near us, beside us (all the various realities), and within us (our inner life).

The existence itself of things, from the smallest to the greatest things, tells us that being is.

This being—which all things have in common and for which they are not simply a nothingness—reveals, in a natural manifestation, that Being which none of them is, but which they all announce. Their becoming, their limits, their very ceasing to exist is the language in which it is stated that the being of all that exists is rooted in a Being that simply and absolutely *IS*. Referring to the sun, St. Francis said, with the language of a poet and the profundity of a mystic: "Bearing thy likeness, O Most High, he points to thee."

This can be an analogy for our inner life. The awareness human beings have had of themselves from the very beginnings of philosophical reflection, especially if enlightened by faith, is the acknowledgment of being. This being is a light and, at the same time, a confession of the Absolute Being, of the most pure Light which knows neither shadow nor error, and which is invoked and sought by the very light that shines forth in the consciousness of human beings, as its guarantee, certainty, and final destination.

So for human beings to say "I" is equivalent to opening oneself to being able to say, in communion with the being of all things, that the Absolute Being is.

And yet, the course of philosophy in the West has witnessed the clouding over of these initial certainties. Consciousness of self has been—and is—lived as negating the objectivity of being. And it has closed itself off from the Absolute Being.

This has led to the great crisis that has marked recent centuries. Now we could ask ourselves: is it true that consciousness of self and being—as the affirmation of reality in itself to the point of acknowledging the Absolute Being—cannot co-exist?

Or rather, are we not called by this very crisis to examine in-depth both the concept of the conscious subject and that of being in all its breadth? And in this way to understand that ultimately the difficulty of our times lies in a reluctance to call upon a new, more fully developed solution, in which the specific gift of Christianity shines forth in all its power? And precisely here Jesus Forsaken presents himself as the master of light, of thought, and—I would dare to say—of *philosophy*.

There may be those who think that to affirm self implies a struggle against all that is not self, because what is not self is perceived as a limit and, what is more, as a threat to the integrity of self. But in that terrible moment of his passion, Jesus Forsaken tells us that though the consciousness of his subjectivity appears to be diminishing as he is, as it were, made nothing, in that very moment it reaches its fullness.

With his being reduced to nothing, accepted out of love for the Father to whom he re-abandons himself ("Into your hands I commend my spirit" [Lk 23:46]), Jesus shows us that I am myself, not when I close myself off from the other, but rather when I give myself, when out of love I lose myself in the other. If, for example, I have a flower and I give it to someone, certainly I deprive myself of it, and in depriving myself, I am losing something of myself (i.e., non-being); in reality, precisely because I give that flower, love grows in me (i.e., being). Therefore, my subjectivity is when it is not, out of love; that is, when out of love it is completely transferred into the other. Jesus Forsaken is the greatest revelation of consciousness, understood as self-affirmation, precisely when he gives himself to the other, to an otherness that, at its greatest extent, in fact, is being. Genuine consciousness of self is born from the communion with being: a communion in which consciousness seems to lose itself but, in reality, it finds itself, it is.

Jesus Forsaken thus enlightens being, revealing it as love. And with this he reveals to us that the Absolute Being is itself love, as affirmed in the first letter of John (see 1 Jn 4:8, 12).

It is love precisely in the dynamic relationship that exists among the three divine Persons, One with the Other, One for the Other, One in the Other. There are three Persons in the most Holy Trinity, and yet they are One because love is not and is at the same time.

In the relationship of the three divine Persons, each one is love, each one is completely, by not being: because each one is, perichoretically, in the other Person, in eternal self-giving.

In the light of the Trinity, being reveals itself, if we can say this, as guarding deep within itself the non-being that is gift of self: not the non-being that negates being, rather the non-being that reveals being as love: *being that is the three divine Persons*.

In the light of Jesus Forsaken the subject, the being of all created things and the Absolute Being itself find a new explanation that can serve as the basis for a new philosophy of being.

This was the hope of great thinkers of our times, like Maritain and Przywara, who foresaw the possibility of progressing in the search for the truth precisely on the basis of the understanding of being as love, as is revealed in the cross of Christ.[1]

---

1. See Jacques Maritain, *Existence and the Existent* (New York: Vintage Books, 1966); and E. Przywara, *Filosofia e teologica dell' Occidente* (Rome: Città Nuova, 1970).

A second point I would like to touch on concerns the significance of creation.

In Hebrew-Christian revelation the world is seen as the creation of God, of a personal God, and therefore destined to have a lasting relationship with him.

Thus, the world has a value in and of itself as well as its own autonomy, which becomes effective in the history of that personal subject which is the human being who has been endowed with the gift of dialoguing directly with God and with other human beings. What is more, the world finds its eschatological fulfillment in the person of the Word incarnate and risen, the only *You* of the Father, who recapitulates all in himself.

Then, according to Revelation, the world should be seen as filled with the presence of God in his Word, through the Spirit.

In the history of Western society, this Christian concept of the world has gradually replaced the mythological vision. In the process, however, the Christian conception has been marked by a cultural crisis that in these times has given rise to various phenomena such as secularism, post-modernism, and the loss of the sacred.

Consequently, we no longer understand how God can fill the world with himself. For people of Western societies, the world has gradually become empty of meaning. And the same holds true, according to some schools of thought, for time and history.

Gone is the intelligence of love capable of grasping the truth and beauty of creation *from its origins*, from God who contains it and nourishes it with himself. Instead, it has been replaced by a skeptical and cold rationality that moves *among* things without penetrating into their deepest roots. The groaning of creation, of which St. Paul speaks (Rom

8:22), seems no longer to be heard. It has been covered by what Heidegger called the "idle chatter of existence," and therefore of an "inauthentic" culture.[2]

Are we up against an irreversible crisis?

Or rather the slow coming to birth of a new world?

Here, too, Jesus Forsaken provides a light for understanding and living the meaning of this drama.

Jesus Forsaken experienced in himself and took upon himself the non-being of all those separated from the source of being: he took upon himself the "vanity of vanities" (Eccl 1:2).

Out of love, he made his own this non-being that we can call negative and transformed it into himself, into the positive non-being that is love, as revealed in the resurrection. Jesus Forsaken made the Holy Spirit overflow into creation, thus becoming "mother" of the new creation. Certainly, this event is *still* in the process of developing: but in the risen Christ, and in Mary assumed into heaven with him, it is already accomplished.

In a certain sense, it is already a reality for the Church, his Mystical Body. If we live in mutual love, which brings Christ among us, and we are nourished by the Eucharist, which makes us become Christ as a community and as individuals, and therefore Church, we can perceive the penetration of the Spirit of God into the heart of all beings, into each one and into the entire cosmos.

And through the Holy Spirit we intuit the existence of a nuptial relationship between the Uncreated and created because in becoming incarnate, the Word aligned himself

---

2. See Martin Heidegger, *Being and Time* (New York: Harper, 1962). This reference cited from G. Reale and D. Antiseri, *Il pensiero occidentale dalle origini a oggie/3* (Brescia: Morcelliana, 1983), 449.

with creation thereby divinizing it and recapitulating it in himself.

This wide and majestic vision makes us think of the entrance of all creation one day into the bosom of the Father.

And we can already see several signs.

For example, when we die and our body is consigned to the earth, if it has been nourished by the Eucharist and therefore Christified, can it not be considered Eucharist for nature? This being the case, our body, although apparently transformed into earth, in reality acts mysteriously as a seed for the transfiguration of the cosmos into "new heavens and new earth" (Is 66:22; 2 Pt 3:13).

Certainly, these new heavens and new earth are still far from their full realization, but we can already see them developing in the heart of creation if we look at it with the eyes of the Risen Jesus who lives in us and among us. This sheds a new light upon and opens up the relationship between people and the world, of which the capacity to transform things through work and technology is just one aspect.

As a result of our experience we feel confident in affirming that the most profound intuitions (whether in the fields of thought, art, science, or of practical projects), when understood in the light of that unity among us by which the presence of the Risen Jesus in our midst makes us participate in his thought (see 1 Cor 2:16), can offer a glimpse into this overflowing of the Spirit of God into all things.

Your Excellencies, ladies and gentlemen, here are a few words about my passionate journey toward Jesus, Word of the Father, and how he, especially in his forsakenness, can be a light for us all.

—Lubich, *Essential Writings*, 209–13

The Charism of Unity and Theology

From an address given during the conferral of an honorary doctorate degree in theology.
(University of Santo Tomas, Manila, January 14, 1997)

A new theology and, at the same time, a new philosophy are emerging from the life of the charism of unity. What are the main points of this theology? Today I would like to recall some of them even if they certainly do not exhaust all the areas of studies and research that are in process. I am referring to God who is love, unity, Jesus crucified and forsaken, and Mary.

First of all, God who is love. Pope John Paul II affirmed that love was the inspiring spark of the spirituality that God has given us.[3] The same can be said of our theology.

Obviously, it is not just any love, but *agape*, God's love, love that is God. Therefore, we could say that the origin of our experience of life and of the theology that emerges from it is the same as that of the Christian faith: "We have known and believe the love that God has for us. God is love" (1 Jn 4:16).

God is Love. The novelty of the Christian revelation is summed up in this confession of faith from the New Testament. It reveals in an unprecedented way the depth of the self-revelation of God in the Old Testament: "I am who I am" (Ex 3:14), and, at the same time, brings those seeds of the Word scattered in the various religions to their unexpected fruition.

Love: not only one of God's attributes, rather his very

---

3. Speech given at the International Mariapolis Centre, Rocca di Papa, near Rome (August 19, 1984), in *Insegnamenti di Giovanni Paolo II*, 1984, vol. VII, no. 2 (Vatican City, 1984), 222–26.

being. And because he is love, God is one and triune at the same time: Father, Son, and Holy Spirit. Jesus reveals that the essence of the Trinity is love and he does so in particular in the moment of his passion. In his passion Jesus arrives at the point of absolute self-annihilation and even death, which then bears fruit in the resurrection and the outpouring of the Spirit.

The Father generates the Son out of love; he "loses himself" in him, he lives in him. In a certain sense he makes himself "non-being" out of love and in so doing he is, he is Father. The Son, who is the echo of the Father, returns to the Father out of love, he "loses himself" in him, he lives in him. In a certain sense he makes himself "non-being" out of love and in so doing he is; he is Son. The Holy Spirit who is the love that circulates between the Father and the Son, their bond of unity, also in a certain sense makes himself "non-being" out of love and thus is; he is the Holy Spirit.

Very closely linked to the first essential point of this new theology is the second: unity.

Since the early days of the Movement Jesus's words in his prayer for unity struck like a bolt of lightning: "That they may all be one. As you, Father, are in me and I am in you, may they also be in us, so that the world may believe that you have sent me" (Jn 17:21).

In attempting to put them into practice, we discovered that these words unleashed a light that illuminated God's design of love for humanity. As we understood it, Jesus is the Word of God made man in order to teach us to live according to the model of trinitarian life, the same life he lives in the bosom of the Father.

He was not content with simply underlining and linking to one another the two fundamental commandments of the Old Testament: "You shall love the Lord, your God, with all your heart, with all your soul, and with all your mind. . . . You shall love your neighbor as yourself" (Mt 22:37–39). Instead, he teaches us the commandment which he himself does not hesitate to call "his" and "new," and by means of which we can live the life of the Trinity here on earth: "Love one another as I have loved you" (see Jn 13:34; 15:12). The commandment of mutual love lived according to the example of Jesus's love for us, to the point of forsakenness that makes us one in him, defines—as the Second Vatican Council also emphasizes—the very vision of humankind that Jesus reveals to us and that is the heart of Christian anthropology.

Therefore, when we live the new commandment, striving to welcome the Father's gift of unity in Jesus, the life of the Trinity is no longer lived only in the inner life of the individual but flows freely among the members of the Mystical Body of Christ.

In this way, the Mystical Body can become in all its fullness what it already is by the grace of faith and the sacraments, in particular the Eucharist: the presence of the risen Christ in history who lives in each one of his disciples and among them (see Mt 18:20).

And now the third point: Jesus crucified and forsaken. It was the Holy Spirit, we believe, before leading us into the mystery of unity, who concentrated our faith and all of our love in Jesus who . . . in an insuperable climax of love and suffering, cries out from the cross: "My God, my God, why have you forsaken me?" (Mk 15:34; Mt 27:46).

In that moment he experienced the most profound separation that can ever be imagined; in a sense, he experienced being separated from his Father with whom he was and remained one. At the same time, he gives all humankind a new and fuller unity than the one lost through sin: he

Spirituality of Communion

reunites all with one another and with God in a new unity, which is a participation in his unity with the Father and with us. Therefore, Jesus Forsaken is the key to understanding and living out unity.

In fact, those who wish to bring about unity must keep in mind and love Jesus Forsaken (right from the very beginning this was the name we gave to Jesus in this mystery that sums up and is central to his redemptive mission). We must love him in a radical way, just as St. Paul who affirmed: "For I resolved to know nothing while I was with you except Jesus Christ, and him crucified" (1 Cor 2:2).

Scripture tells us that in his forsakenness Jesus made himself "sin" (see 2 Cor 5:21), "cursed" (see Gal 3:13) in order to make himself one with those who are far from God.

This is why Jesus Forsaken seems to be the God of our times. He is heaven's response to the terrible chasm of sufferings and trials cut deep into the hearts of men and women by the atheism permeating many aspects of our modern culture; by the extreme poverty of millions of displaced people; by the quest for meaning and ideals of the disillusioned and confused new generations.

Jesus Forsaken is the God of our times also because he is a reflection of the division that exists between the Churches, a division that today we are more conscious of than ever.

But precisely discovering his face in these divisions gives us the hope that we can make a vital contribution to the process of reunification. In particular we have the sense that Jesus Forsaken "who, though he was in the form of God . . . emptied himself," as Paul writes (Phil 2:6–7), has opened a providential way for dialogue with the faithful of the religious traditions of the East, one of the more difficult and pressing frontiers at the dawn of the third millennium.

And finally, Mary. We feel that she cannot be considered merely as one point of our theology among many, even if an important one. For many reasons: perhaps because our Movement is her work, the Work of Mary; perhaps because many signs of the times and official statements by the Magisterium indicate the emerging "Marian profile" of the Church; perhaps because we are witnessing the surprising phenomenon of the figure of Mary being recognized by other religious traditions, we foresee the heralding of a new and original season of reflection on the person of Mary. And we believe that this reflection should explore Mary's role in the context of God's universal design of salvation for all of humanity and the cosmos. In fact, as John Paul II recently said, Mary is "an integral part of the economy of communicating the Trinity to mankind."[4]

She is the mother of the Word of God made man, which places her in a unique and extraordinary relationship with all the persons of the Holy Trinity (see Lk 1:35).

This, above all else, is Mary's true greatness, which "magnifies" the greatness of God and his works.

But Mary is also the mother of the Church. She generated the Son of God in the flesh by the power of the Holy Spirit. Likewise, sharing as no one else in the redemption through her desolation at the foot of the cross (see Jn 19:25–27), she shares in a real way in the regeneration of the children of God that the Holy Spirit has brought about in the womb of the Church. Having fully carried out God's design for her, Mary now lives in heaven. She is the flower and the first fruit of the Church and of creation, which in her is already Christified and divinized. In a certain way, we can think of her as being set into the Trinity, through grace, the icon and expression of all creation. In fact, since in God there is

---

4. "Mary's Relationship with the Trinity," in *Insegnamenti di Giovanni Paolo II*, 1996, vol. XIX, no. 1 (Vatican City, 1998), 47.

a perfect perichoresis[5] among the three divine Persons, and because, through Christ, in the Spirit, there is also a perichoresis, the mutual indwelling of the Persons of the Trinity, brought about between the Trinity and humanity, apex and synthesis of creation: "You ... loved them even as you loved me" (Jn 17:23)—all creation, recapitulated in Christ, is also destined to be, as Mary already is, eternally set into the Trinity: that is, to live and rejoice infinitely in the intimate life of God, in the ever new and unending dynamism of the trinitarian relationships.

We have the impression that, as I hope to have shown, the doctrine that emerges from this charism of unity sheds a new light on the core of revelation. Our theologians, in fact, quoting von Balthasar, recall that: "Charisms such as those of Augustine, Francis, Ignatius can receive, as gifts of the Spirit, glimpses into the center of revelation that enrich the Church in very unexpected and yet everlasting ways. They are always charisms in which intelligence, love, and discipleship are inseparable. Here we realize that the Holy Spirit is at once divine wisdom and divine love, and is never simply pure theory but must be lived out in practice."[6]

Above all, these theologians point out that those who study this doctrine have the possibility of participating in Jesus, or as St. Augustine says,[7] of becoming one with him. And this is perhaps because in constantly striving to live according to this charism of unity, they remain united in the name of Jesus, and therefore he is present among them; and also because they are nourished daily by Jesus-Eucharist.

---

5. The mutual indwelling of the Persons of the Trinity.

6. *Teologica* (Milan, 1992), 22; see *Theo-Logic* (San Francisco: Ignatius Press, 2000).

7. See Saint Augustine, *Commentary on the Gospel of John*, Homily 21, 8–9.

Therefore, one of the novelties that seems to emerge from this charism lived out in this way is that the theology derived from it is not just a theology regarding Jesus, but rather a theology of Jesus: of Jesus present in and among theologians.

In fact, they point out that up until now in Christian reflection the predominant approach has been to look at Jesus as the "object" of theological study. Obviously, there was always the awareness that such an "object"—the Son of God made man—required an adequate knowing subject, that is, reason illuminated by faith, a Christified reason.

In the past, nonetheless, particularly in the recent past, the theology elaborated by most theologians of Western cultures was thought of primarily as a reflection on God and on Jesus rather than as a participation, through faith and love, in Jesus's knowledge of the Father. Of course there are, just to take Western examples, some exceptions among theologians who had gifts of the Spirit and often were saints, such as Anselm of Canterbury, Bernard of Clairvaux, Thomas Aquinas, Bonaventure, and even earlier, in both the East and West, the Fathers of the Church. But, in general, it was a knowledge sought almost "from outside" rather than from within the mystery being considered. Instead, as Jesus said: "No one knows the Son except the Father, and no one knows the Father except the Son and anyone to whom the Son chooses to reveal him" (Mt 11:27).

Jesus gives this knowledge to his Mystical Body by way of the Spirit. And it is received in all its fullness when we are "one" in him (see Gal 3:28), almost one "mystical person."[8]

Thus, through this charism of unity, the necessary condition is present for the rebirth of a great theology of Jesus:

---

8. Thomas Aquinas, *De veritate*, 29, 7–11.

clearly not the Jesus of two thousand years ago, but the Jesus who lives today in the Church.

And from this discovery comes a second novelty. Given that this theology is a theology *of* Jesus, who has ascended to the bosom of the Father and who lives today in unity which is the Church, it sees things from a new perspective: the viewpoint of the *One*, in other words, from God, where everything is in its true reality.

Therefore it is "one" perspective, side by side with others and so not excluding them; on the contrary it presupposes them and gives them value. But at the same time, it could also offer them a unique contribution. It could integrate them and lead them to unity, thus opening new horizons for them. Furthermore, since in a certain sense, as we already mentioned, it is a theology of Jesus, in whom all created realities are recapitulated, it could also shed light on the various sciences, making them truer and more genuine. In fact, we could hope to see theology return to being the mother of all sciences and even their queen—different from the sense this had in the Middle Ages—not destroying their legitimate autonomy, but leading them back to their true root and their true purpose.

—Lubich, *Essential Writings*, 204–20

The Charism of Unity and Education

From an Address during the Conferral of an
Honorary Doctorate in Education
(The Catholic University of America,
Washington, DC, November 10, 2000)
As I have said on other occasions, our Movement can also be viewed from a theological, philosophical, cultural,

social, economic, or pedagogical perspective, as well as from an ecumenical or inter-religious one. Let me share with you now some of the ways that the more significant points of this spirituality have had an impact in the area of education.

In fact, our Movement and the various stages of its development can be viewed as one continuous, extraordinary educational event. All the necessary factors are present, including an educational theory and a well-defined teaching method that underlies our efforts to educate. But first let us ask ourselves: what is education? Education can be defined as the itinerary that a subject (either singly or as a community) pursues with the help of one or more educators, moving toward a goal considered worthwhile both for the individual and for humanity. What then are the characteristic elements of our educational method, which emerge from the main points of the spirituality we live?

Let us consider the first point: the "revelation"—if I may use this term—of God as Love. We see that from the beginning of our Movement there has been only one *educator*, the Educator par excellence: God who is Love, God who is our Father. It was he who took the initiative. *With the intentionality* characteristic of a true educator, he has accompanied us, renewed us, and given us new life along an intensely rich itinerary of formation, both personal and communal.

He has enabled us and countless others to rediscover the true meaning of the greatest Fatherhood there is: a discovery of enormous importance, considering the various attempts in Western culture to affirm—on theoretical and practical levels—that "God is dead." There has been an eclipse of God's Fatherhood that has also contributed to an eclipse of the father figure, causing a loss of authority on the level of human and educational relationships. This has led to a moral relativism and an absence of rules in the life of the individual, as well as in interpersonal and social relationships. This often leads to grave consequences such as violence and the like, as if to agree with Dostoyevsky that "killing God is the most horrific form of suicide"... and "If God does not exist, then everything is permitted."

We have had the grace to come to know God. God is Love, and certainly not a distant judge, or a jealous enemy who uses his power to destroy us, or who does not take care of us. On the contrary, he is an educator who acknowledges each person's unique and distinctive identity, extolling the human being. He loves human beings, and this is why he is also demanding. As an authentic educator he demands and educates people in responsibility and commitment. God is love. For this reason he freed us from the greatest slavery of all, and re-opened the doors of his home to us. And we know the price his Son paid for our ransom. No educator has ever considered human beings as highly as a God who died for them. God who is love has raised each and every human person to the highest possible dignity: the dignity of being his child and heir. Each and every person!

It was precisely upon this understanding that we are all children of the same father that Comenius,[9] that great figure in modern educational theory, based his core idea: we must "teach everything to everyone."

Another key point of our spirituality is the Word of God.

"Teach everything to everyone." But in order to do so, one must use—as Comenius himself said—the educational

---

9. Comenius (1592–1670), an important figure in the Reformation, was from Moravia (in the present-day Czech Republic). Among his interests was education, and he attempted the first systematic understanding of pedagogy as a science.

principle of proceeding step by step. Thinking about it now, it seems that the Father suggested this method to us from the very first days of the Movement. He prompted us to live his word, choosing one sentence at a time from the gospel each month to be put into practice in our daily lives.

But this immediately gave us "everything," because Jesus is present in his entirety in each word of the gospel (and when we live his word, he lives in us). At the same time, we were like children being nourished on his word; and the more we were clothed in it, the more we grew into adults in faith and in life.

Through this very simple educational technique, which combines proceeding step by step with imparting knowledge in full, the light of this Ideal of life has spread and continues to spread far beyond the Movement as a powerful spiritual and educational experience that is constantly expanding.

The uniqueness of the word of God lies in its being *the word of life*, a word that becomes experience in a world frequently tarnished, even in education, by an abundance of empty words.

And we have experienced the power to educate, to offer alternatives, to challenge carried by this word, which is always alive and always new. Bit by bit, as it was impressed upon our lives, it gave them (and this is the tremendous task of education) an *existential unity*. This unity helped us overcome the fracturing and fragmentation that people often experience in relation to themselves, to others, to society, to God, while at the same time drawing out the originality, the unrepeatable uniqueness of each person.

Precisely because of this *existential unity* between word and life, between saying and doing, many people have found our experience credible and convincing. This experience provokes profound changes in people on an existential level, thereby setting in motion a true educational process. The will of God is another point of our spirituality.

Faithfulness to the word of God also taught us to "put aside our base will," all those desires that still tie us to the narrow behavioral patterns of the self-centered "I." It helped us instead to follow the will of God, which leads us to transcend ourselves continually, in a movement beyond "I" to "you" that enriches us and makes us free.

As a rule, in the moral education of a person, one gradually moves from a necessary initial phase of dependency (*heteronomous morality*) to the *autonomous morality* that should characterize a mature adult subject. In our experience, too, we observe a movement from an initial adherence to the will of another and to his law (manifested in many ways)—which we grab on to like a *child* trusting completely in the guidance of an adult—to a powerful sense of freedom, the result of having made this Law *our own*. We then feel that it has become our law, that it has become so much a part of us that we feel *adult* precisely because we are able to say: "It is no longer I who live, but Christ who lives in me" (Gal 2:20).

And then another point: Jesus who cries out, "My God, my God, why have you forsaken me?" (Mt 27:46; Mk 15:34). Jesus Forsaken is our secret, our key idea, in education as well. He points to the "limit without limits" that should characterize our educational work, demonstrating the extent and intensity it must have.

But who is this Jesus Forsaken whom we have decided to love in a preferential way? He is the figure of those who are ignorant (his ignorance is the most tragic, his question the most dramatic). He is the figure of all who are needy, or maladjusted, or disabled; of those who are unloved, neglected, or excluded. He personifies all those human and social situations, which more than any others cry out for education in a special way. Jesus Forsaken is the paradigm of those who, lacking everything, need someone to give them everything and do everything for them. Therefore, he is the perfect example, the ultimate measure of the learning subject, who manifests the educator's responsibility. He indicates to us the "limit without limits" of the need for education, and at the same time, the "limit without limits" of our responsibility to help and to educate.

However, Jesus Forsaken—who went beyond his own infinite suffering and prayed: "Father, into your hands I commend my spirit" (Lk 23:46)—also teaches us to see difficulties, obstacles, trials, hard work, error, failure, and suffering as something that must be faced, loved, and overcome. Generally we humans, whatever our field of endeavor, seek to avoid such experiences in every way possible. In the field of education, as well, there is often a tendency to be overprotective with young people, shielding them from all that is difficult, teaching them to view the road of life as smooth and comfortable. In reality, this leaves them extremely unprepared to face the inevitable trials of life. In particular, it fosters passivity and a reluctance to accept the responsibility for oneself, one's neighbor, and society that every human being must assume.

For us, instead, precisely because of our choice of Jesus Forsaken, every difficulty is to be faced and loved. And thus *educating to face difficulty*—which involves commitment on the part of both the educator and the one being educated—is another key idea of our educational method. There are two other points that I would like to consider: unity and Jesus in our midst.

Spirituality of Communion | 131

In order to do so we should ask ourselves the following question: what is the aim of this educational process?

We share the same goal as Jesus. We could define it as his goal in educating: "May they all be one": therefore, unity—a profound, heartfelt unity, of all human beings with God and with one another. Unity is a very timely aspiration. Despite the countless tensions present in our world today, the entire planet, almost paradoxically, is striving toward unity. Unity is a sign and a need of our times.

However, this drive toward unity within people—as the etymology of the word "education" (Latin *e-ducere*: "draw forth") indicates—must be drawn out in a positive way. This implies, on all levels of human endeavor, an educative process consistent with the demands of unity, so that our world will not become a Babel without a soul, but an experience of Emmaus, of God with us, capable of embracing the whole of humanity. This might seem a utopia. But every authentic educational approach includes a utopian thrust, that is, a guiding principle that stimulates people to build together a world which is not yet a reality, but ought to be. In this perspective, education can be viewed as a means for drawing nearer to this utopian goal.

In our approach to education, in which the spiritual and the human penetrate one another and become one (through the incarnation), this Utopia is not a dream, nor an illusion, nor an unattainable goal. It is already present here among us, and we see its fruits when we live out Jesus's words: "Where two or three are gathered in my name, I am there among them" (Mt 18:20).

Education's goal, its highest aim, becomes a reality.

In this we experience the fullness of God's life, which Jesus has given us, a trinitarian relationship, the most genuine form of social relationship, in which a wonderful synthesis is achieved between the two goals of education: to teach the individual and to build the community. We believe that our experience of this trinitarian, communitarian spirituality brings to fulfillment many ideas held by outstanding men and women throughout the history of education, whose initial premises were often different from ours, but who insisted on the importance of education in building a society founded on truly democratic relationships. One example among many would be the great contribution offered by John Dewey to education throughout the world, beginning with the United States. We also find many similarities in the recent concept of "service-learning," which affirms that the formation of the person should also involve a formation in and for the community.

Of course, our experience of community life is based on Jesus's invitation: "Love one another as I have loved you.... Be one" (see Jn 15:12; 17:21). This motivation is religious in nature, but it has extraordinary effects in the field of education.

The goal that has always been assigned to education (*to form the human person, so as to render him or her independent*) is implemented, almost paradoxically, by *forming the person-in-relationship*, which for us means *the human person in the image of the Trinity*, one who is capable of continually transcending self in the context of the presence of Jesus in our midst. It is through this spiritual and educational practice *of mutual love*, to the point of becoming completely one—a practice followed by all the members of the Movement, since all are called to live this communitarian experience in small groups—that we work toward the achievement of the *goal of all goals*, expressed in Jesus's prayer and testament: "May they all be one." As instruments under his guidance, we want to spend our lives for the fulfillment of this goal, which is at one and the same time a utopia, and a reality. It is through this educational process that we as individuals and as community become capable of meeting with, entering into dialogue with, and working together with other persons, other Movements, and so on. And it is also through this in-depth educational process that, with God's grace, we can aspire to personal and communal sanctity.

Mary is an exceptional example of one who has put all the educational points I have mentioned into practice in her life.

Of course, Jesus is the one who fully lived out this pedagogical itinerary, in the dynamics of an experience that fully included both the life of the Trinity and his forsakenness on the cross. In his earthly experience, he lived interpersonal relationships with exceptional intensity, expressing empathy, acceptance, and hope, and experiencing the struggle involved in educating, as well as a life of unity with the Father and with "his own." Clearly he is the most genuine and demanding witness of what it means to be an educator.

—Lubich, *Essential Writings*, 219–24

The Charism of Unity and Communications

From an Address to the Conference
"Communication and Unity"
(Castel Gandolfo, Italy, June 2, 2000)
The mass media, apart from being the marvelous phenomenon we all know, and that in a certain way mark our times, have a particular resonance and are of fundamental importance in our Movement, both in its development and now.

The connection between the media and the Focolare Movement
In effect there is a twofold affinity between the Movement and the media that prompts me to say something. First of all, they share similar goals. The purpose of the Focolare Movement is to share in bringing about what our young people have called the *dream of God*, that is the fulfillment of Jesus's heartfelt request to his Father just before he died: "May they all be one" (see Jn 17:21).

And what is the goal of the mass media? Its collective vocation is obvious: it too works to bring people together.

But it is not just the goal for which the Movement works that links the mass media so closely to our way of living. There is a second kind of affinity, one related to methodology. The *spirituality of unity*, which is characteristic of the Movement, is not practiced on a purely personal dimension; it is communitarian, collective. In the development of mass communication we can see a new step in the evolutionary plan for humanity. This development introduces into it, we could say, an unstoppable movement from complexity to unity, a movement in real time from fragmentation to the search for oneness.

The Means of Communication and the Focolare Movement

The "new media"—The beginning and development of our using the so-called "new media" really deserve a separate chapter. Here again, it all started with life. In 1952 we were given a wire recorder and a little later a home movie camera. They were small events. . . . I remember we said: "The spiritual step we are now taking here should be made at the same time by all our members even to the ends of the earth."

This desire to share everything, this fire of communion, over the years led to two audiovisual centers. Dedicated to

Saint Clare (patroness of television), they have multiplied in many other countries. These centers produce audio and video material, two useful means of communication continually updated as technology advances. The *broadcast media* too, with generous help from several public telecommunications entities, are employed more and more by the Movement, especially for large international events.

As I said, our "media" arose from practical circumstances, little things, like the desire to stay in contact or the need to update those not present for events we considered important, or the duty to give spiritual support to those in difficulty.

For many years we did not publicize the Movement and its extraordinary spread, so what we have now has come not so much through the deliberate effort of the Movement as it has happened spontaneously.

What is important for us is that everything continues to develop out of life, even as we are ever more convinced that the media are, so to say, *made especially for us*, since their purpose is to bring people together in unity. Be that as it may, we realize that the first Christians did not have the media. Their hearts overflowed with the message of Christ, and they passed it from mouth to mouth until, as Tertullian said, though they were born "yesterday" they had already encompassed the earth. Jesus used his voice. He wrote nothing, except in the sand.

A Look at Worldwide Communication Today

A rapid overview of modern means of communication cannot fail to reveal that along with the swift development that day by day renders them more useful and fascinating, they also seem to present a series of major new problems for societies, families, and individuals.

It offers a panorama of lights and shadows.

To cite just some of them: *globalization* which risks homogenizing cultures and suffocating the wealth of their diversity; *ethical relativism* which mixes messages of substance with what is biased, partisan, or superficial; *turning life into a spectacle* which exploits suffering and private life; an atmosphere of *excessive competition* among the providers of the means of communication; the exaggerated *invasion of public space*. . . . How to use the media without being used?

Lights and shadows, I said. . . . The media today are either accepted uncritically or blamed for promoting immorality, violence, and superficiality or overvalued as infallible instruments of power, almost new idols for a humanity without other certainties. We know they are simply tools, but let us appreciate all their "enormous untapped potential," to use an apt expression of Pope John Paul II.[10] We would like and would encourage everyone to use them well, faithful to the prophetic message they contain.

The Universal Movement toward Unity

Their message is "unity." Here I would like to offer great thanks to God for the way in which he is not absent even from modern discoveries and new technologies, for the way in which he guides history.

And so it is that at this precise moment when humanity seems to wander in darkness after the collapse of powerful ideologies and the obscuring of so many values, and on the other hand at this precise moment when there is a yearning for a world that is more united, for universal brotherhood, at this precise moment we find in our hands these powerful

---

10. From a message to a group of Polish bishops, February 14, 1998. *Insegnamenti di Giovanni Paolo II*, 1998, vol. XXI, no. 1 (Vatican City 2000), 269–81.

means of communication, a *sign of the times* that says "unity." Do we not see the finger of God in this?

The apostle Paul, the first Christian who in a hostile culture had the courage to make himself, so to speak, *the means of communication* for the message of Christ, were he alive today, would certainly have used the media. At Athens he took the floor in the Areopagus (see Acts 17:22), which was in some way the TV of the day. As John Paul II has said: "The means of social communication are indeed the new 'Areopagus' of today's world—a great forum which, at its best, makes possible the exchange of truthful information, constructive ideas, and sound values, and so creates community." And as he said in the same address: "It is the task of communication to bring people together and enrich their lives."[11]

At the root of communication—One of you asked me a question: "How do we achieve such communication? What is the basis for a communication that enriches and unites humanity?"

I am not an expert in the media, as I am not in many other fields, but I would reply with St. Paul: "For I decided to know nothing among you except Jesus Christ, and him crucified" (1 Cor 2:2). I would add: "crucified and forsaken," according to the particular aspect of Jesus's passion that has been revealed to our spirituality.

Perhaps in him we can find an answer, even if our hearts waver and our minds are bewildered upon merely touching the remarkable similarities between the Son of God, who is the Word, and the subject of communication. Jesus was a great communicator: "Never has anyone spoken like this!" (Jn 7:46); "All the people were spellbound by what they heard" (Lk 19:48), his contemporaries acknowledged.

---

11. Message of the Holy Father for the XXXII World Communications Day, no. 5, May 24, 1998.

Let us linger for a moment on his final personal experience. Jesus ended his earthly existence by being killed in the most shameful way possible in his day (crucifixion, reserved for slaves), a punishment that also meant separation from the community, rejection, erasing any social and religious belonging for the condemned person.

The *great communicator*, who had captivated the crowds, now found himself alone, betrayed, ignored: "I do not know this man" (Mk 14:71), said his chief disciple. But that was not all. Even God the Father, who he said knows all that is hidden (see Jn 5:20) and whose relationship had always supported him, seems to break off all communication. This "forsakenness" is certainly the darkest night, the most dreadful agony. He cries: "My God, my God, why have you forsaken me?" (Mt 27:46).

His cry, which sums up the nothingness of all things, has always accompanied the human story. We can cite here two iconic images that certainly are fixed in our memories. Who does not recall the agony of *The Scream*, the painting by the Norwegian Edvard Munch, symbol of the isolation of a human being without relationships? Or the terror caught by a reporter's casual snapshot of the little Vietnamese girl, Kim Phuc, wrapped in napalm flames as she fled screaming from her scorched land, the very image of humanity as a child torn from its roots? These appalling signs draw us back to the abyss of forsakenness experienced by Christ the Word who cries out at the silence, at the "absence" of God.

Jesus crucified and forsaken, the mediator (the *medium*) between humanity and God, who, when the last separation has collapsed, when unity has been achieved, disappears and becomes nothing, is a terrible and fascinating mystery. He is an infinite void, almost the pupil of God's eye, window through which God can look at humanity and humanity in a certain way can see God. He spoke, lived, and worked, and taught for three years, and his words, spoken "for all time" were then and will be for all eternity "the way, and the truth, and the life" (Jn 14:6). Yet our faith teaches us that his being "himself" reached fulfillment at the moment of his most total gift, when he offered his life in the way just described.

So we can ask ourselves, was his cry at the ninth hour his fullest expression as the Word? Was it, so to speak, the height of his communication? Yes. And it is in this self-annihilation in the abyss of individuality, where every relationship is dead, that he gives us the gift of his reality as *person*, capable of meeting God and other creatures. Precisely in giving himself without limit he reveals himself as Word, infinitely communicating himself and introducing us into the mystery of redemption and of the life of God, into the vortex of love among Father, Son, and Holy Spirit.

If every human relationship reflects and follows the pattern of the trinitarian relationships, how can communication, another word for human relationship, avoid this dynamic, this law inscribed in its DNA?

New People for a New Communication
The things I have said so far are only intuitions prompting further research in communications, which would involve various disciplines, beginning with theology. It is research still to be done, or better, still to be lived.

It is unthinkable that a *new communication* be imposed from above, by some international agency or institution. It will come rather from the experience of communicators who have God-Love as a model for communication and as a paradigm for professional relations.

—Lubich, *Essential Writings*, 290–95

Toward an Economy of Communion

From an Address during the Conferral of an Honorary Doctorate in Economics
(Sacred Heart Catholic University, Piacenza, Italy, January 29, 1999)

Typical of the Focolare Movement is what we call the "Economy of Communion," a unique manifestation of a free economy based on solidarity. This authentic expression of the spirituality of unity in economic life can be understood in its entirety and its complexity only if viewed within the vision this spirituality has of the human person and social relationships. It originated in 1991, in Brazil, where the Movement has been present since 1958. It later spread to all of that country's states, attracting people of every social category.

For a number of years, however, I had realized that given the rapid growth of the Movement (in Brazil there are approximately 250,000 members of the Focolare), despite our communion of goods, it was not possible to meet even the most urgent needs of some of our members.

It seemed to me, then, that God was calling the Movement to something more and something new.

Although I am not an expert in economic issues, I thought that our people could set up businesses that could tap their expertise and resources to produce together wealth for the benefit of those in need. They would have to be managed by competent persons capable of making them function efficiently and deriving profits from them.

These profits would then be put in common.

One part would be used for the same goals as the early Christian community: to help the poor by providing for their needs until they found work. Another part, to develop structures to form "new people" (as the apostle Paul calls them), that is, people formed and animated by love, capable of living out what we call the "culture of giving." The last part, of course, would be used for the growth of the company.

Throughout the world our Movement has more than twenty "little towns" that witness to the gospel. They are modern communities with all the features of modern society, and therefore they need to have businesses alongside schools of formation, homes for families, a church, handicrafts, and other activities that have sprung up to provide a livelihood for their inhabitants. With this new development of the Movement, in these towns real industrial areas were to come into being.

This idea was welcomed enthusiastically, not only in Brazil and in the rest of Latin America, but also in Europe and other parts of the world. Many new businesses sprang up and several existing businesses joined in the project, modifying their methods of management.

Today some 654 companies and 91 cottage industries are involved with this project. It includes enterprises operating in different economic sectors, in more than 30 countries: 164 in the tertiary sector, 189 manufacturing firms, and 301 providers in the field of social services.

The experience of the Economy of Communion, drawing on the specific characteristics of the spirituality that inspired it, takes its place alongside the numerous initiatives by individuals and groups that have sought and seek to "give a human face to the economic system." It joins those frequently little-known entrepreneurs and workers who envision and live out their business dealings as something more than and different from the pursuit of sheer material gain.

In fact, as in many other economic activities motivated by an aspiration for the ideal, the people involved with this project—entrepreneurs, managers, employees and others connected somehow to the various businesses—take as their primary commitment to focus their attention, in all aspects of their activity, on the needs and aspirations of the person and on advancing the common good. In particular, they strive to:

- establish loyal and considerate relationships based on a sincere spirit of service and cooperation with clients, suppliers, government offices and also with competitors;
- appreciate the employees, keeping them informed and involving them in different ways in the management of the business;
- maintain a way of doing business inspired by a culture of legality;
- pay special attention to the working environment and respect for nature, even if these require considerable added costs;
- work together with other local business and social concerns while keeping in mind the needs of the international community, with whom they feel a sense of solidarity.

The Economy of Communion project also has other characteristics with great significance for us because they are linked more directly to the view of the world that comes from our spirituality. Here are some of them:

1. Those working in Economy of Communion companies strive, while acting in accordance with the practices required by productive organization, to make this aspect of their life consistent with everything else they do. In fact, we are convinced that it is necessary to let the values we believe in shape every aspect of social life, and therefore also economic life, so that it too can become a field of human and spiritual development.

2. The Economy of Communion proposes ways of acting inspired by free service, solidarity, and concern for the most needy—ways of acting usually considered typical of non-profit organizations—to for-profit enterprises as well. The Economy of Communion, therefore, is not so much a new type of enterprise, alternative to those that already exist. Its aim is rather to transform from within usual business structures (be they public ownership, cooperative, or other), establishing all relationships inside and outside the business in the light of a lifestyle of communion. And all this is done respecting in full the genuine values both of business practice and of the market (those highlighted by the social doctrine of the Church, and in particular, by John Paul II in *Centesimus annus*).

3. Those in economic difficulty, recipients of one part of the profits, are not viewed merely as dependents or beneficiaries of the enterprise. Instead they are essential members of the project within which they make a gift to the others of their needs. They too live the culture of giving. In reality, many of them choose to give up the help they are receiving as soon as they regain a minimum of financial independence and often they share with others the little they have. All of this reflects the fact that, while promoting a culture of giving, the Economy of Communion is not based upon the philanthropy of a few, but rather upon sharing, where each one gives and receives with equal dignity in the context of a relationship of genuine reciprocity.

4. The enterprises of the Economy of Communion, besides resting upon a profound understanding among the people who run them, feel themselves part of something much larger. They share their profits because they are already experiencing communion. For this reason—as I mentioned earlier—the enterprises develop within small

(at least for now) industrial parks near the little towns of the Movement, or if geographically distant, linked "ideally" to them. Many ask how enterprises can survive in the marketplace when they are so attentive to the needs of all the people they deal with and to the good of the whole of society.

Certainly, the spirit that animates them helps them to overcome those internal conflicts that hinder and in some cases paralyze all human organizations. Furthermore, their way of doing business inspires the trust and goodwill of clients, suppliers, and investors.

We must not forget, however, another essential element: Providence. It has constantly accompanied the development of the Economy of Communion throughout the years. Space is left in the enterprises of the Economy of Communion for God's intervention even within the hard facts of economic reality. And every time they choose to go against the trend that commonly accepted business practices would advise, they have experienced that God never fails to supply the hundredfold promised by Jesus: some unexpected revenue, an unforeseen opportunity, the offer of a new joint venture, the idea for a successful new product.

This, in a few words, is the Economy of Communion.

—Lubich, *Essential Writings*, 274–77

The Charism of Unity and Psychology

From an Address during the Conferral of an Honorary Doctorate in Psychology
(University of Malta, February 26, 1999)

Our Movement can be considered from a psychological perspective as well as from theological, philosophical, and educational points of view.

In order to understand the contribution that it brings to the field of psychology, we need to refer back to the main points of our spirituality.

The first point is God who is love.

Psychology tells us that every person has a basic need to be recognized as a unique individual with one's own identity and to not be considered as simply a number or an object.

Under normal circumstances, this sense of security comes from parents, from family, from personal talents, or from education, which establish a sense of identity, of being distinct from others. But all of these things can be compromised. Others may not acknowledge one's identity, or may not understand or appreciate it, leading a person into feelings of insignificance and into depression.

But each person's discovery of and achieving certainty that he or she has been wanted and is loved by God—not abandoned to chance or blind fate—is the basis for having that psychological stability which gives a meaning to life and a purpose in the world.

Only the awareness that God is love-for-the-person-too gives him or her the strength to continue going outside self, to live, to love, and to create communion in society.

Another point of this spirituality is doing God's will.

We know that the psychic development of a person (of the self) begins in the early stages of "narcissism" in which one is concentrated exclusively on self and on one's own needs and pleasures. Then, little by little, the person's field of relationships opens up to include members of the family, and later on, the school environment and society. According to Igor Caruso, eventually these relationships should open up to a transcendental "You," after overcoming the final obstacle that stands in the way of reaching full maturity: one's own self.

In other words, freeing the self from all internal and external conditioning and, in the end, recognizing the inherent relativity of the self (which implies ceasing to defend it and to place it in opposition to God and to others) means accepting oneself without masks, in order to bring the individual will into conformity with a transcendent will.

In this lies human perfection as well. Because if God's will is to love one's neighbor, "to make yourself one" with a neighbor means to give up defending the self in order to go beyond self into the other and, ultimately, into the Other ("You did it to me").

It has been said: "Those people who have reached self-fulfillment, basically, are capable of deeper interpersonal relationships than are others. . . . They are more capable of losing themselves in others, of a greater love, of identifying themselves more perfectly with others, of eliminating the obstacles set up by one's ego than other people find possible."[12]

Then there is love and mutual love.

The affirmation that God is love, and that his will coincides with love, in other words, with loving one's neighbor, is confirmed not only by Jesus's teachings but also by the psychological experience of interpersonal relationships. Only relationships that are not violent or controlling but instead recognize and respect the other's "person" as a transcendent being are relationships that "love the other as oneself." Not only does my love acknowledge the other person as a being who is distinct from me, equal to me, and transcendent like me, but this same love also affirms my own "existence."

---

12. Abraham H. Maslow, *Motivation and Personality* (New York: Longman, 1987), 271–72.

Only love takes into account our diversity (or distinction) while, at the same time, safeguarding our equality, and therefore making unity possible. The novelty of the culture brought by Jesus lies precisely in the fact that he revolutionized interpersonal relationships. Before his coming, relationships among people were governed by family ties, social class, particular interests, or merely external goals. With Jesus, all these motivations become less important because one becomes aware that one has an intrinsic transcendent value, in fact, that one represents God himself for others: "Just as you did it to one of the least of these who are members of my family, you did it to me" (Mt 25:40). The psychological relevance of this dynamic is obvious. For example, if we take it to its extreme consequences, then I am most fully a person when I freely and consciously affirm the other even at the cost of my own life. This dynamic is expressed by Jesus in these words: "No one has greater love than this, to lay down one's life for one's friends" (Jn 15:13).

Said in another way: no one affirms the self, is so truly a person, as does the one who denies self and thus transcends self in order to save the transcendence of the other (and we have luminous examples in Jesus, Father Maximilian Kolbe, Mother Teresa). This is the most authentic "humanism" imaginable and achievable.

Jesus crucified and forsaken.

The psychological law of personal development is also defined by the spiritual law that Jesus announced: "Those who love their life lose it, and those who hate their life in this world will keep it for eternal life" (Jn 12:25). In fact, in the process of growing to maturity, one cannot reach a new stage without becoming detached from and renouncing the one reached previously. For example, weaning is a painful passage for a child, but it is essential for progressing toward adulthood; accepting the arrival of a new sibling is another painful passage, from the egotistical position of being the center of attention to a stage of socialization, the relativity of self, to become integrated with others, transcending self in the "we."

It is generally accepted that all psychological illnesses actually are born from the refusal of the suffering inherent in this passage (because a person would rather remain comfortable in a familiar situation), for fear of all that is "new" or of the "others" who are seen as enemies who can limit or even take away my identity.

When, in fact, in order to safeguard the self we refuse to enter into communion—because we are afraid of being made a thing subject to someone else's will, exploited, objectified, squeezed dry, swallowed-up by others, as psychologists say—psychologically (and also spiritually) we are already dead.

According to Carl Jung, the one who expressed the highest point in the achievement of personhood was Jesus, who cried out on the cross: "My God, my God, why have you forsaken me?" (Mt 27:46; Mk 15:34). In the very moment when God experiences human mortality, his human nature reaches the divine.

Living the word and imitating Mary are two other key points of the spirituality of unity.

Those who live the word give witness to the fact that the authentic person is simple and because simple, he or she is also free. All forms of attachment, whether to self or to things destroy the self, fragment it, both because attachments nurture pride and self-satisfaction and because they fabricate that "false self" which psychologists call the ego.

The problem people face today is the need to rebuild an integrated self, freeing it from the propensities of the ego, that is to say, freeing it from all forms of greed and possessiveness. For the one who has an integrated self knows how to empty the self, to strip self of everything in order to be enriched by communion with others.

And this is precisely what the gospel teaches.

Mary is the icon of this self-emptying, above all in her desolation at the feet of her crucified son whom she loses. But into that immense emptiness enter all the children of God.

And at the end, unity.

Psychologically speaking, it is impossible for individuals to have a "sense of identity" if there are not others who recognize them as subject. Psychologists of all schools agree that human beings need to reaffirm one another in their individuality through genuine interactions and contacts. In fact, in order to be able to be a gift for the others, first one must feel and be recognized as being "different" from the others.

But in order to be a personal gift it is necessary to enter into communion with others.

And herein lies the difference between so-called "interest groups" and the Christian community as Jesus intended. An interest group is made up of individuals who come together with a particular goal in mind (athletic clubs, civic, political or religious associations, trade unions, schools, study groups . . .) and whose interaction is limited to carrying out those common interests. As for all that falls outside the realm of such common interests, these individuals remain closed in on themselves.

The Christian community, instead, is not formed for reasons that are external to the nature of community, but as a result of the very character of love which creates communion.

And experience confirms that this type of community is possible. Clearly the motivation to bring about such a community comes from Jesus's invitation: "Love one another as I have loved you . . . that they may all be one" (see Jn 15:12; 17:21). Obviously this is religious in nature. But the psychological effects are extraordinary: each one, being a relationship of love with others, as a consequence becomes fulfilled as an authentic person. This, briefly, is our spirituality of unity seen from a psychological perspective.

—Lubich, *Essential Writings,* 225–29

The Movement for Unity in Politics

Address to the First Conference of the Movement for Unity in Politics of the Focolare Movement (Castel Gandolfo, Italy, June 9, 2000)

We are here today to open the International Congress of the Movement for Unity in Politics: an important step toward defining its identity, the ideals it pursues, its methods, and its goals.

It is a fairly new Movement. In fact, its origins date back to May 2, 1996, on the occasion of a meeting I had with a group of politicians in Naples, Italy. But its roots sink deep into the history, spirituality, and doctrine of the Focolare Movement that promotes it. Indeed, we have always given special attention to the world of politics because it offers us the possibility of loving our neighbor in a crescendo of charity: from interpersonal love to an ever-greater love toward the *polis*. Many of our people have committed themselves in politics on various levels, often holding positions of responsibility.

Today, I would like to go over with you those events in our history that have had the greatest influence on the formation of our political thought, underlining in each of them what retains lasting value and, from my viewpoint, what it might contribute to the heritage of the Movement for Unity in Politics. In 1948, in the Chamber of Deputies,[13] we first met the Honorable Igino Giordani, a prominent person with extensive cultural, social, and political experience. He was an active figure during the first years of the difficult postwar period, a scholar, and a reference point for the generations that longed for freedom during the years of dictatorship. Giordani was a cofounder of the Focolare Movement, and for us, he has always represented, due to a special plan of God, the dimension of humanity, with its history, its sufferings, its achievements, its quest for an authentic ideal.

He opened our heart to humanity, to its problems and concerns: the rebuilding of Italy and the rest of Europe in the wake of World War II, the rise of democracy, the division between East and West. In turn, from the spirit of the Movement Giordani received a new stimulus for his own political activity. We can see this in an address he made on universal peace, applauded by the entire Italian Parliament; the first bill on conscientious objection, presented together with the Socialist Calosso; his dialogue on peace with the Communist Laiolo.

Within a short time, a small but significant group of politicians began to gather around Giordani. They shared our ideal of life and sought to live it in Parliament.

There, for the first time in a political setting, they experienced the "art of loving" that I spoke about a few months ago on a special occasion in Campidoglio.[14]

---

13. The Chamber of Deputies is the legislative house of the Italian Parliament. The title "Honorable" indicates that Igino Giordani was a member of Parliament.

14. When Chiara Lubich was made an honorary citizen of the city of Rome on January 22, 2000.

It is an art that requires that we love *everyone*, without exception, regardless of their party affiliation; that we be *the first to love*; that we *make ourselves one* with them in order to welcome them, emptying ourselves of all our worries and thoughts.

Christians are the first, but not the only ones, called to live this art of loving: *everyone can and must love*. It is a law for believers of all traditions of faith. In fact, it is written in the DNA of every human being.

Consequently, if love becomes mutual, according to Jesus's commandment, "Love one another as I have loved you" (see Jn 13:34), Jesus himself is present among us. In fact, Jesus promised us: "For where two or three are gathered together in my name [in my love], I am there among them" (Mt 18:20). It is a presence of Jesus that transforms people individually and creates unity among them. It is not simply an agreement of opinions or choice to follow a certain course of action based on the same political choice. Instead, this human-divine unity bonds people in a deeper way, beyond differences of culture and political affiliation. On the foundation of unity, differences acquire their true meaning, and in mutuality, they become enrichment for one another.

Therefore, the basic principle is to live first of all as true Christians and then as people engaged in politics.

In view of the fact that people of other religions and cultures also participate in the Movement for Unity in Politics, the same commitment can be formulated as follows: first, be people who believe in profound and lasting human values, and then take political action.

Just as the presence of Jesus among us, the effect of unity, is the heart of all our communities, it is likewise the heart of our political communities. Already in 1962, Tommaso Sorgi, a Member of Parliament, sensed the urgent need for this presence.

He wrote to me from the Chamber of Deputies: "Those of us who live at the very core of this 'blessed' public life continually experience that, on a purely human level—even on the level of the most noble ethical values—there is not the slightest hope of redemption for this narrow-minded world full of insincerity, conflicts, and power struggles. And, unfortunately, we find that not even religious values are able to change the *homo politicus*, who accepts them only as long as they are expedient, and then sets them aside when they no longer serve his or her purposes. Individual efforts alone . . . seem to be insufficient. We need a lightning bolt of wisdom to reawaken all of humanity."[15]

And we can receive this light of wisdom especially from God present in Jesus who is drawn by our mutual love. He himself comes among us wherever we are engaged, and through us, takes political action. This was the purpose of the group of politicians in our "parliamentary cell." Its members, who after a while came from different parties, have changed since 1950, but not its goal: *since our unity makes it possible, to bring Jesus into Parliament.*

The presence of Alcide De Gasperi was also noteworthy because it underlined the political significance that our Movement could have. De Gasperi, like the first men and women Focolarini, was originally from Trent and was very close to the Movement.

He knew the spirituality of unity quite well. In fact, it fascinated him and reinforced his vocation to unity, that same vocation which eventually made him, together with

---

15. T. Sorgi, Letter to Chiara Lubich, February 7, 1962. Unpublished document.

Adenauer and Schuman, a founder of the European Union. In fact, a documentary on the life of De Gasperi points out how, especially in the final years of his life, all of his thoughts seemed to come together in Jesus's testament: "May they all be one"—the same Jesus whose name he invoked three times before dying.

Our contacts with De Gasperi made us realize how much a politician who loves his country can accomplish and how much that love can cost him. At a certain point, we began to correspond with one another. In one of my letters to him from 1950, I had written: "You are as important to us as is Jesus among us, because we are convinced that all authority comes from God.

"You have all the grace of state necessary to govern Italy. . . . You should be the best and brightest expression of your own party and of the parties of others."

This letter provides an opportunity for me to speak about the view that we have had of authority from the early years of the Movement.

We know that it is God who gives authority to human beings as his delegates in the world, an authority that should be used as an instrument of truth and love (see Jn 19:11). For this reason we have always had *the highest respect for authority*.

However, it is an authority given by a God who is Love and is Trinity and therefore takes on a meaning not always easily found in political theories and codes of law. For us, authority participates in the love of the Creator for each created being. It is the love of a Father for each and every person, even the weakest and most insignificant, who nevertheless bear in themselves the undeniable dignity of being children of God.

This authority given by God to every human being (see

Gn 2:28–29) is then the source of the specific partaking in this authority conferred upon political leadership for the government of the "city of Man."

However, it is important to keep in mind the great, the tremendous responsibility that those who govern have before God and before the people. We must never forget that citizens are the first partakers in God's love for the city. They have a role to carry out in conscience and each one possesses inalienable rights and duties. Each citizen is an active subject in the political community, not simply a passive object, and is called therefore to behave accordingly. Political power must put itself at the service of the citizen, as we hear so often from all sides.

But in order that this may be accomplished ever more fully, the political activity carried out by those who govern, as a service of truth and love, must be met by an ever-growing participation of its citizens in public affairs as an expression of the authority they have received from God. Only in this mutuality is it possible to build the well-being of the whole community.

This dynamic of mutuality reminds us of the trinitarian relationship of the two parts, a harmonious relationship of unity in multiplicity. In the Movement we certainly do not want to confuse religion and politics, as has happened and happens as a result of the extremist tendencies of some Christians and also non-Christians. It is necessary to recognize the precise role politics plays in society with its specific expertise.

On the other hand, Jesus is Life, and he is Life in all its fullness. He is not only a religious fact. To separate Jesus from the wholeness of the life of human beings is a real modern-day heresy. It makes people slaves to something beneath them, relegating God the Father to a place far from his children. No, he is *the Man*, the perfect Man who sums up in his person all men and women and every truth and drive that they may feel, in order to be raised to their rightful place.

At times it is thought that the gospel does not resolve all human problems and that, instead, it simply brings about the kingdom of God understood in a strictly religious sense. But it is not so. Certainly, it is not the historical Jesus who resolves today's problems. It is Jesus-us, members of his Mystical Body, Jesus-me, Jesus-you. . . . It is Jesus present in each person, in that given person—when his grace and love live in him or her—who constructs a bridge or builds a road. It is Jesus, the true and most profound personality of every person. And it is as another Christ that the Christian brings his or her characteristic contribution to all fields, whether in science, in art, in politics. Our politicians' sense of commitment took this direction, and in 1959 the *St. Catherine Center* was founded for them.[16] Renewed in the spirit of unity and reinforced by an ever-deeper understanding of the principles of Christian social doctrine, for almost ten years this Center was the point of convergence for their many aspirations and concerns and the point of departure for their activities.

For the St. Catherine Center, however, political responsibility was not exhausted simply in the pursuit of the common good of citizens from a purely material point of view, which for the most part is useful. It had to work also toward building a society that is open to achieving more noble goals. Politics was seen as having the possibility and the duty to encourage all individuals to assume their respon-

---

16. The St. Catherine Center was a gathering of politicians, facilitated by Igino Giordani, who sought to bring Christian principles into their parliamentary work.

sibilities as members of a body, the body of the whole of humanity, and to offer them the opportunity of reaching that self-fulfillment in this world and that happiness which is possible only in the context of universal brotherhood.

In addition, they also emphasized how Christians should never forget that what they accomplish, in common purpose with all those who seek the good of humanity, builds up the earthly city and thus continues the work of God the creator. At the same time, their work brings closer the "new heavens" and the "new earth" (see 2 Pt 3:13) because together with the cosmos, Christ has redeemed all human activity. Therefore, if these works are completed in conformity with the commandment of love, they will endure.

What is more, while broadening the commonly accepted view of political commitment and encouraging its members to set their daily choices in a wider historical perspective, the St. Catherine Center also examined, in the light of the truth present in the human heart, all the political laws that have withstood the test of time in order to confirm their validity. And our people involved in politics did not feel alone; they sensed the active presence and help of those who throughout the course of history have contributed to accomplishing the same objective. Moreover, they studied new laws inspired by relationships of mutual love among persons, among groups and among peoples.

There has always been a further conviction, confirmed and rediscovered in new forms every day, that the Providence of God is never lacking, but acts in human affairs and also, therefore, in political matters.

These are some of the ideas that the Movement for Unity in Politics has inherited from the St. Catherine Center.

But one basic idea lies at the foundation of everything and guarantees the success of our politicians as they continually strive to live the ideals they pursue. We offer it to those of you who are Christians, but not only, because Christ died for all people.

We have already affirmed that one must, first of all, be an authentic Christian and, on this foundation, carry out one's activity in politics. Very well, to be an authentic Christian means to follow Christ by living what we have called "the art of loving," but also, as he himself said in powerful words, by denying oneself and taking up one's own cross.

One's own cross.

What is the specific cross of those who move and work in the political world today? I think it is often the lack of unity, of harmony, that makes their task heavy and not very fruitful; the rigid and opposed positions between parties without understanding the others' motives; the divisions caused by clashes among ethnic groups within nations, divisions between nations. . . . We need to find the way to overcome these disunities, to restore unity. Jesus himself came on earth to restore the unity that had been lost between humanity and God and of men and women with one another. He accomplished this through his passion and death, and above all—this is the conviction of theologians and saints—when he experienced within himself the greatest possible disunity: the disunity between himself and the Father with whom he was one. And he cried out: "My God, my God, why have you forsaken me?" (Mt 27:46).

This mystery is the key that opens the way to unity for the members of the Focolare Movement, and therefore also for that specific expression of the Movement, the Movement for Unity in Politics.

Only those who keep the image of Jesus crucified and forsaken ever before them, who recognize his face in every division, who love him and know how to embrace the cross

Spirituality of Communion | 159

of division out of love for him, are capable of recomposing unity.

And in loving Jesus crucified and forsaken they receive the gift of a light that the mind does not produce on its own and a strength that is more than common.

We have always been aware, since the earliest days of our Movement, that the charism of unity also contains its own culture. On the one hand, it is the offspring of Christian tradition, but at the same time, it is new, because it is enlightened by this charism. But it was the growth of the people of unity, the spreading of their Ideal outside the structures of the Focolare Movement, that highlighted the specific characteristics of this culture and that led to the studying of its doctrine: in theology, philosophy, politics, economics, psychology, art, and so forth.

And now the latest innovation: the encounter between the people of unity and its doctrine has given rise to what we call "inundations" or "torrents of living water," using an expression taken from St. John Chrysostom. In other words: the development of authentic new movements, particularly in the field of economics, through the Economy of Communion, and in politics, continuing the work of the St. Catherine Center, through the Movement for Unity in Politics.

Thus the Movement for Unity in Politics is bringing about a new political culture.

But its vision of politics does not give rise to a new party. Instead, it changes the method of political activity: while remaining faithful to his or her own genuine ideals, a politician of unity loves everyone, as we said, and therefore in every circumstance searches for what unites.

Today we would like to present a vision of politics perhaps as it has never before been conceived. We would like to give life—forgive my boldness—to a politics of Jesus, as he considers it and where he acts through each of us, wherever we are: in national and regional governments, in town councils, in political parties, in various civic and political groups, in government coalitions and in the opposition. This unity lived among us, then, must be brought into our political parties, among the parties, into the various political institutions and into every sphere of public life and into the relationships among nations.

Then the people of all nations will be able to rise above their borders and look beyond, loving the others' country as their own. The presence of Jesus will become a reality also among peoples and states, making humanity one universal family. It will be a family that goes beyond a limited concept of international society, because within it relationships among persons, groups, peoples are conceived of in a way that dismantles all types of divisions and barriers.

This is the goal of the Movement for Unity in Politics which is beginning to blossom all over the world. It is a Movement that is capable of giving rise to new political projects and that appeals to politicians at every level and position. Through their profession and social commitments, members of the Focolare Movement are present in it, together with many others who know the Ideal of unity and live it, without necessarily belonging to the Focolare.

Now, in order to have a better understanding of this Movement let us look more closely at what is specifically characteristic of it.

We know that the redemption brought about by Jesus on the cross transforms from within all human bonds, imbuing them with divine love and making us all brothers and sisters.

This has profound meaning for our Movement, if we consider that the great political plan of modernity was the attainment, as summarized in the motto of the French Revolution, of "liberty, equality, fraternity." While the first two principles, however, have been partially achieved in recent centuries, despite numerous formal declarations, fraternity has been all but forgotten in the political arena.

Instead, it is precisely *fraternity* that can be considered as *the hallmark of our Movement*. What is more, by living out fraternity, freedom and equality acquire new meaning and find greater fulfillment.

In order to conclude this part of my talk, I would like to explain now the importance that the figure and role of Mary have had in the history of our Movement.

In 1959, as was customary during those years, all the people of our community spent their summer holiday together. During that time, in the little town of Fiera di Primiero in the Dolomite Mountains, some twelve thousand people from twenty-seven countries came and went. And in a solemn act, representatives of these nations consecrated themselves and their nations to Mary. Members of parliament who were present consecrated also their political commitment to her.

Why this special love for Mary, and why do we consider her as the Queen of all nations and leader of our Movement?

Mary is the one who sings: "The Mighty One has done great things for me" (Lk 1:49). God has placed his plan for humanity in her; in her he reveals his mercy for humankind, destroys the false projects of the proud, casts down the powerful from their thrones and lifts up the lowly, reestablishes justice and redistributes riches.

Who, then, is more a politician than Mary?

The task of the Movement for Unity in Politics is to contribute toward fulfilling in human history what Mary announces as already accomplished in herself.

—Lubich, *Essential Writings* 236–47

Unity with Other Christians

Address to the Second European
Ecumenical Assembly
(Graz, Austria, June 23, 1997)

"Reconciliation: gift of God and source of new life" is the theme of this Second European Ecumenical Assembly—reconciliation in the widest sense of the word.

In first place, the kind that has priority: reconciliation with God.

Then reconciliation among the Churches in order to reach visible unity; then, further, reconciliation with other religions insofar as it is possible through dialogue; and also reconciliation among cultures, among peoples; and between the human race and nature. . . .

In this talk I want before all else to give thanks to God for his free gift. Without it we could not even speak of unity.

Then I want to consider the reconciliation that the Holy Spirit has inspired among the Churches. He is the one at the origins of the vast ecumenical movement, which has shown thus far an unexpected vitality throughout the world. He has brought about prayer groups, activities of all kinds, new institutions, special structures and Movements in various Churches and ecclesial communities. But I will dwell on one detail of the whole ecumenical movement.

As you know, Christ founded his Church as one and only one, which all Christians in the world profess in the Nicene-Constantinopolitan creed: "We believe in one, holy, catholic and apostolic Church."[17]

There is only one Church of Christ, therefore. It is entered by baptism, which is "the sacramental bond of unity

---

17. See the World Council of Churches, Faith and Order paper 153, *Confessing the One Faith* (Geneva: World Council of Churches, 1991).

existing among all who through it are reborn."[18] We know, however, that it is not enough only to be united spiritually in a common baptism. "The ultimate goal of the ecumenical movement is to re-establish full visible unity among all the baptized."[19]

This seems to me to emphasize the fundamental role of ecclesiology.

Indeed, it is so.

But what kind of ecclesiology do we mean?

Cardinal Willebrands was almost prophetic when he wrote that "a deeper ecclesiology of communion may offer perhaps the great opportunity for the ecumenism of tomorrow. The restoration of the unity of the Church should be sought in the light of this ecclesiology, which is at the same time very ancient . . . and very modern."[20]

Today the ecclesiology of communion (*koinonia*) is accepted in the theological dialogues among the Churches as the way to understand the Church and ecclesial unity: "The Church finds its proper model, its proper origin and its proper fulfillment in the mystery of the one God in three persons."[21]

But then we come to the pressing question: is there something that can make these new ecclesiological insights work?

In this regard the World Council of Churches and others are seeking an ecumenical spirituality.[22]

---

18. Pontifical Council for Promoting Christian Unity, *Directory for the Application of Principles and Norms on Ecumenism*, 92.

19. John Paul II, *Ut unum sint*.

20. "Avenir de l'ecumènisme," *Proche Orient Chrètien* 25 (1975): 1, 14–15.

21. The Catholic-Orthodox Dialogue, "Il mistero della Chiesa e dell'Eucaristia alla luce del mistero della Santa Trinità" in *Enchiridion Oecumenicum*, vol. 1, 2190.

22. See Consultation on "Christian Spirituality for Our Times," World Council of Churches, Iasi, Romania, May 1994.

An Italian Waldensian pastor said that "the lack of an ecumenical spirituality renders our task much more difficult and demanding."[23]

An ecumenical spirituality, therefore, a spirituality of communion.

But is such a spirituality within reach today?

We can take into consideration that there exist praiseworthy efforts toward this goal. Perhaps they are known, perhaps they are not, because serious things, the things of God, usually grow in silence.

But if they are the work of the Spirit, then unity is not just a dream or a utopia. It is a real possibility.

We can ask ourselves, however: what are the fixed points, the indispensable principles for an ecumenical spirituality worthy of the name?

Since the Church is not something just human but divine, a first key point cannot but be: God, and, given that this spirituality is a spirituality of communion, God understood as he is, is Love (see 1 Jn 4:8).

If now at the dawn of the third millennium we Christians take a new look at our two-thousand-year history and especially that of the second millennium, we cannot but be saddened by the succession of misunderstandings, struggles, and confrontations which often ripped apart the seamless robe of Christ, which is his Church.

Who was at fault? Certainly there were historical, cultural, political, geographical, and social circumstances.... But there was also a deterioration among Christians of their characteristic unifying element: love.

Exactly so.

---

23. R. Bertalot, "La riconciliazione nei dialoghi fra le Chiese," in *Studi Ecumenici* 14, no. 3 (1996): 354–60, 359.

So now, in trying to put right all that was wrong and to find new strength to start again, we must turn our attention to the very source of our common faith, to God-Love, the great revelation of the Christian mystery. In these times it is God-Love who, in some way, must reveal himself anew to our hearts as individual Christians and to the Church that we compose. First of all to each one of us. For how could we think of loving others in order to bring about reconciliation, if we do not feel loved profoundly, if we Christians do not have in ourselves the certainty that God loves us?

The fact is that while we know by faith that God is Love, we often do not think of it and live as if we were alone on this earth, as if there did not exist a Father who looks after us in everything and through everything; who counts even the hairs on our head, who knows everything about us; who wants to make everything work together for our good—the good that we do and the very evil he permits.

To begin living a spirituality of reconciliation effectively in the Church and the world today, we need to be able to repeat, with full conviction and in truth, the words of John the evangelist: "We have known and believe the love that God has for us" (1 Jn 4:16).

But he does not love us only as individual Christians, he also loves us as Church. And he loves the Church for when in history it has acted according to God's plan for it. But also—and here is the wonder of God's mercy—he loves it inasmuch as it has not lived up to his plan, in Christians being divided, if however they now seek full communion in his divine will.

It is this extremely consoling conviction that led John Paul II, trusting the One who draws good out of evil, to reply as he did to the question, "Why did the Holy Spirit allow all these divisions?" While admitting that it could have been because of our sins, he said: "Could it not be that these divisions have also been . . . a path continually leading the Church to discover the untold wealth contained in Christ's gospel and in the redemption accomplished by Christ? Perhaps all this wealth would not have come to light otherwise."[24]

Believing, therefore, in God who is Love for us and for the Church; this is the starting point.

But if God loves us we cannot remain immobile in the face of such divine benevolence. Like true children we must reciprocate his love, and here too both as individuals and as Church.

As individuals by acting as Jesus did: wanting the will of the Father in place of our own, repeating with Jesus: "My food is to do the will of him who sent me" (Jn 4:34)—that divine will which is written, we know, in holy scripture, especially the New Testament.

For those who wish to commit themselves to reconciliation, it is a duty and therefore a key point for any possible ecumenical spirituality, to live the words of the gospel, one by one, to re-evangelize our way of thinking, of seeing, of loving.

Cardinal Bea used to say that the more Christians live the word, the more it makes them similar to Jesus and therefore more similar to one another and more united.

Christians should make the words of holy scripture their own, especially the New Testament, and in particular the one that sums up the law and the prophets: fraternal love.

The only genuine Christian reconciler will be the one who knows how to love others with the very charity of God,

---

24. John Paul II, *Crossing the Threshold of Hope* (New York: Doubleday, 1994), 167.

which brings Christ to light in each person, which goes out to all (Jesus died for the whole human race), which always takes the initiative; that charity which makes us love each person as ourselves, which makes us one with our brothers and sisters, in suffering, in joy. . . .

And the Churches too should love with this love.

"That the love with which you have loved me may be in them, and I in them" (Jn 17:26), Jesus prayed. And we instead are always ready to forget his testament, to scandalize the world with our divisions, a world we should be winning for him.

Over the centuries every Church, in some way, has turned rigid through waves of indifference and misunderstanding, if not of mutual hatred. What is needed in each Church is a supplement of love. Indeed, the Christian world needs to be overwhelmed by a torrent of love.

Love, therefore, mutual love among Christians, mutual love among Churches. That love which leads to putting everything in common, each a gift to the others, so that we can foresee the future Church with one truth, one truth alone, but expressed in different ways, seen from different perspectives, made beautiful by the variety of interpretations.

In his book *Crossing the Threshold of Hope* John Paul II writes: "It is necessary for humanity to achieve unity through plurality, to learn how to come together in the one Church, even while presenting a plurality of ways of thinking and acting, of cultures and civilizations."[25]

It is not that one Church or another must "die" (as at times it is feared), but that each Church should be born anew in unity.

And living in this Church in full communion will be

---

25. John Paul II, *Crossing the Threshold of Hope*, 167.

marvelous, as fascinating as a miracle, and will excite the attention and the interest of the whole world.

Mutual love, however, is true to the gospel and genuine when it is practiced in the measure Jesus desired: "Love one another as I have loved you. No one has greater love than this, to lay down one's life for one's friends" (Jn 15:12–13).

But in what way did Jesus die?

In his passion and death he did not suffer only during the agony in the garden, the scourging, the crowning with thorns, the crucifixion, but also in that climax of his suffering when he cried: "My God, my God, why have you forsaken me?" (Mt 27:46). And this suffering, as theologians and mystics affirm, was his greatest trial, his deepest darkness.

Now, it seems that to build communion up to the full in mutual love requires today that we contemplate and mirror in ourselves that particular suffering.

And it makes sense.

If Jesus was called to remedy the sin of the world and therefore the division of people cut off from God and in consequence disunited among themselves, he could not have fulfilled his mission without experiencing in himself the extreme depths of separation: that of himself, God, from God; feeling himself abandoned by the Father.

Jesus, however, re-abandoning himself to the Father ("Into your hands I commend my spirit" [Lk 23:46]), overcame that immense suffering and in this way brought human beings back into the bosom of the Father and into a mutual embrace.

But if this is so, it will not be difficult to see in him, precisely in him, the brightest star that must light up the path of ecumenism; the pearl we must find to bear great fruit.

An ecumenical spirituality will flourish to the degree that those dedicated to it see in the crucified and abandoned Jesus, who re-abandons himself to the Father, the key to understanding every disunity and to recomposing unity. A productive ecumenism demands hearts touched by him, that do not evade him, but understand him, love him, choose him and know how to see his divine face in every disunity they meet. And they find in him the light and the strength not to stop in trauma, in the fracture of division, but always to go beyond and to find a solution, the complete, achievable solution.

Mutual love leads then to realizing unity.

And unity cannot but be another key point of an ecumenical spirituality. Jesus, before being crucified, before being forsaken by the Father, prayed a long prayer for unity: "Father, may they all be one" (Jn 17:21).

And unity, lived out, has an effect which is also, so to speak, a *pièce de résistance* for a living ecumenism. We are speaking here about the presence of Jesus among people united in his name. As Jesus said: "Where two or three are gathered in my name, I am there among them" (Mt 18:20).

The Fathers of the Church often based their explanation of Jesus's presence in the Church on two passages: "Where two or three . . . ," which I have just quoted, and "I am with you always, to the end of the age" (Mt 28:20).

Living with Jesus in our midst, present through mutual love, we enter more fully and livingly into the presence of Jesus in the Church.

And this is already a powerful bond! It is a help on the path to visible unity! Jesus between a Catholic and an Evangelical who love one another, between Anglican and Orthodox, an Armenian and a Reformed. . . . It is a gift that also makes less painful the time of waiting until we can all share in one Eucharist.

Another key point must be a great love for the Holy Spirit, Love personified. Jesus gave him to us as he breathed his last on the cross. He filled the Church at its birth with him at Pentecost.

It is the Holy Spirit who binds in unity the Persons of the Holy Trinity, and the Holy Spirit is the bond of the members of the Mystical Body of Christ.

In the reconciliation among us Christians, then, we must not forget Mary, whom a Council we share, the Council of Ephesus, proclaimed Mother of God, *Theotokos*.

Mary, precisely because she is Mother, can do much for unity. And not only under that title; she is the perfect Christian. As infant, fiancée, spouse, virgin, mother, and widow, she can be a model for Christians, who are called to become more perfect Christians (see 2 Cor 13:9–11). Clothed in the Word of God, icon of the gospel lived, she is our "form." And under the cross, more than anyone else, she is able to be for us an example of one who can repeat: "In my flesh I am completing what is lacking in Christ's afflictions" (Col 1:24) in the effort to work and suffer for unity.

An ecumenical spirituality lived in this way can produce exceptional fruits.

But we become aware that it will have one effect above all. Since it is communitarian it will bind into one all those who live it, so that they will feel solidarity among them and already be, in a certain way, one. They will be conscious of forming, we might say, a single Christian people which, with all that is happening as a result of the other forces inspired by the Spirit in this ecumenical age, can be leaven for the full communion among the Churches. It will be in effect the implementation of another dialogue, added to

Spirituality of Communion

the dialogues of charity, prayer, and theology: the dialogue of the people. A people formed not only of laity, but of the whole people of God.

A dialogue more than urgent and timely if it is true, as history shows us, that little is certain in the ecumenical field when the people are not involved. A dialogue that will lead to our discovering with greater clarity, with greater interest, and to our valuing all the immense heritage already common to Christians, made up of baptism, holy scripture, the first Councils, the Fathers of the Church . . . and will make us live it together.

We are waiting to see this people, already appearing here and there, and we wish to wonder at it wherever there is a Church. . . .

A spirituality of communion, then.

Unity is the distinctive feature that sums it all up.

If we put it into practice we will see the world go in reverse, like a film running backwards.

By what dramatic divisions, by what disintegration, by what crises is our planet pervaded, our planet which is immersed even now in indifference, in secularization, in materialism.

With this new life we can turn back, while still going forward. Humanity will find again the unity for which God created it and the Churches will live in full communion in the way that he planned and founded his Church.

It is worth trying, therefore. And may this Second European Ecumenical Assembly be the opportune moment.

—Lubich, *Essential Writings*, 325–33

The Focolare Movement's Experience of Interreligious Dialogue

From an Address to an Interreligious Seminar
The Initiatives of Change Center
(Caux, Switzerland, July 29, 2003)

The first major experience we had with brothers and sisters of other religious faiths was with the Bangwa, a tribe in Cameroon, which followed a traditional religion. They were almost on the point of extinction from high infant mortality when we began to assist them.

One day their king, the Fon, and thousands of his people were gathered, in a large clearing in the middle of the forest, for a celebration in which they offered us their songs and dances. All at once I had a strong impression of God, like a huge sun, embracing all of us, we and they, with his love. For the first time in my life, I intuited that soon we would be involved also with people of non-Christian traditions.

The event that in some "founded" this dialogue occurred at London in 1977 during a ceremony conferring the Templeton Prize for Progress in Religion. I gave a talk, and when I was leaving the hall, the first to greet me were Jews, Muslims, Buddhists, Sikhs, Hindus. . . . The spirit of Christianity that I spoke of had so impressed them, that it was clear to me that we would have to be involved not just with our own and other Churches, but also with these brothers and sisters of other faiths. So began our interreligious dialogue.

Two years later, in fact, came the meeting with a distinguished Buddhist, the Rev. Nikkyo Niwano, founder of the Rissho Kosei-kai, who invited me to Tokyo to speak about my spiritual experience to ten thousand Buddhists. So began between the Focolarini and followers of the Rissho

Spirituality of Communion | 173

Kosei-kai a great spirit of fellowship wherever we happen to meet.

But the most surprising meetings with Buddhism were with some eminent representatives of Thai monasticism.

During a long visit to our international little town of Loppiano in Italy, whose eight hundred residents try to live a life faithful to the gospel, two of them were touched profoundly by the unity among everyone and by a Christian love they had never before experienced.

That reduced the prejudices that were preventing a true dialogue between them as Buddhists and us as Christians.

These monks returned to Thailand and lost no opportunity to tell thousands of the faithful and hundreds of monks about their encounter with the Focolare Movement. So began, if we may call it this, a Focolare-Buddhist Movement, that is, of one of Buddhists and Christians, one part of the relationship of fraternity we are building in the world.

Later we were invited to Thailand to speak at a Buddhist university and in a temple to monks, nuns, and many laity.

Their interest was remarkable and we were edified by their asceticism and their detachment from everything, so characteristic of them.

And the dialogue with Islam?

There are now 6,500 Muslim friends who belong to our Movement, and what binds them to us is the spirituality, which gives a spur and an affirmation that leads to a more profound and vital adherence to the essentials of their own Islamic faith. We have had many meetings with our Muslim friends. What characterizes these gatherings above all is the presence of God which one notices when they pray, and which gives much hope.

I saw this hope become a reality in the Malcolm Shabazz Mosque in Harlem (USA) six years ago when I was invited to explain my Christian experience to three thousand African American Muslims.

Their welcome, beginning with that of their leader, Imam W. D. Mohammed, was so warm, sincere, and enthusiastic that it led us to great expectations for the future.

I returned three years ago to the United States, to Washington, to make a presentation about our working together before a large convention of seven thousand Christians and Muslims. In an atmosphere of the greatest elation and accompanied by endless applause we exchanged a sincere embrace, promising each other we would continue our journey in the fullest union possible and spread it to others. So now there exist yet more portions of fraternity.

I cannot fail to mention the increasingly frequent meetings with Jewish sisters and brothers in the state of Israel and elsewhere. The most recent for me was in Buenos Aires with one of their larger communities, a meeting then followed up on various occasions by other members of our Movement. Deeply moved, we exchanged a pact of mutual love. It was so profound and heartfelt that it made us feel we had suddenly overcome centuries of persecution and misunderstanding.

In the last three years we have begun a promising dialogue in India with the Hindus. We have strong fraternal contacts with the Gandhian Movements in the south of this vast country. A profound dialogue has begun at Mumbai with professors from Somaiya University and from the Indian Cultural Institute. More recently a relationship has begun with a very large Movement, Swadhyaya, which shares our goals of brotherhood and unity in diversity.

A year ago we had our first Hindu-Christian symposium. The atmosphere was so beautiful and inspiring that we were able to share with them many truths of our faith.

We had the impression of a horizon that we never imagined opening before us.

A few months ago I returned to India, and we were able to continue this dialogue at a level of spirituality which, in the words of the authorities of the Church I belong to, "is the summit of the various forms of dialogue and responds to the deepest expectations of people of goodwill."[26]

Now we are planning other similar symposia, Buddhist-Christian and Muslim-Christian.[27]

With the expansion of our Movement, we are in contact with all the principal religions in the world, and approximately thirty thousand members of these religions share, as far as they are able, the spirituality and goals of the Movement.

Our interreligious dialogue has developed so rapidly and fruitfully because the decisive and characteristic element has been the art of loving, of which I spoke previously.

The Golden Rule fosters a climate of mutual love in which you can establish a dialogue with your counterparts. In this dialogue you try to make yourself nothing in order, as it were, to enter into the others.

To "make yourself nothing" means the same as to "make yourself one" with others.

In these two simple expressions, which I already referred to, lies the secret of a dialogue that can build unity.

"Making yourself one" is not a tactic or an external way of behaving. It is not just an attitude of goodwill, openness,

---

26. Personal letter from Archbishop Michael Fitzgerald, February 28, 2003.

27. In the years immediately following this talk, other symposia were held. In 2004 at Castel Gandolfo, Rome, there was the first Buddhist-Christian symposium, and in the year after that the Muslim-Christian and Jewish-Christian symposia took place. The second Buddhist-Christian symposium was at Osaka and Mount Hiei, Japan, in 2006.

and respect, or an absence of prejudice. It is all that, but it is something more.

This practice of "making yourself one" requires that we empty the ideas from our mind, the affections from our heart, and everything from our will in order to identify with the other. We cannot enter into the soul of our brothers or sisters to understand them, share their sorrow or joy, if our own spirit is rich with a preoccupation, a judgment, a thought . . . with any other thing. "Making yourself one" demands spirits that are poor, poor in spirit in order to be rich in love.

And this most important and indispensable attitude has a double effect. It helps us become enculturated in the world of others, thus getting to know their culture and customs, and disposing them to hear what we have to say. We have noticed, in fact, that when people see someone dying to self in order to "make him or herself one" with others, they are struck by this and often ask for an explanation.

Then we can pass on to "respectful proclamation."[28] Being true to God, to ourselves, and being sincere with our neighbor, we share what our faith affirms on the subject we are discussing, without imposing anything, without any trace of proselytism, but only out of love. This is the point at which, for us Christians, dialogue opens itself into proclaiming the gospel. Our work with many brothers and sisters of the major religions and the brotherhood we experience with them has convinced us that the religious pluralism of humanity can lose much of its negative value as an instigator of divisions and war so as to acquire in the awareness of millions of men and women a sense of challenge: that of restoring unity to the human family, because the Holy Spirit is present and active in some way in every

---

28. See *Novo millennio ineunte*, §56.

religion, and not just in the individual members but also within the religious tradition itself.

Speaking about the remarkable event at Assisi, John Paul II defined it as the "marvelous manifestation of the unity that binds us despite our differences and divisions."[29]

Let us fill our hearts, then, with genuine love. With this we can hope all things for unity among the believers of the world religions and for a brotherhood that is lived out in the whole human race.

—Lubich, *Essential Writings*, 344–47

The Abba School

In the past years of the life of the Movement—and now we will speak of the cultural aspect of the Movement—its ascetic and mystical aspects have been giving life to a doctrine. It is a doctrine well rooted in the eternal truth of divine revelation, which, however, develops and renews the theological tradition. The presence in the Movement of Bishop Klaus Hemmerle, a well-known, profound, and modern German theologian, now deceased, and of men and women scholars in secular or religious disciplines who are part of the Movement and who have studied all their life and with the passing of years have become enriched with a true and profound cultural experience enlightened by the charism of unity, offered the possibility of starting a school which would study this doctrine. It is called the Abba School. . . . The experience made during these years is now studied, situating it in the context of Scriptures and the great tradition

---

29. "Assisi, Giornata Mondiale di Preghiera per la Pace," October 1986, in *Insegnamenti di Giovanni Paolo II*, IX, 2 (1986), Vatican City 1986, 1252–53.

of the Church. Intuitions or illuminations which the Spirit seems to have given us concerning the vast panorama of faith are studied in depth. The characteristic of this school, however, is that the professors put unity at the basis of their studies. Every time they meet, they renew their commitment to a mutual love that is expressed through their listening to one another with total attention. This brings Jesus's presence among them. Something else that is new is emerging from the charism lived in this way. Here knowledge flows not from without, but from within the mystery which is studied, that is, through the participation, in faith and love, in the knowledge that Jesus has of the Father. Moreover, because here it's a matter of a theology which in a certain way we could call a theology of Jesus, in which all created realities are recapitulated in him, man and God, this theology sheds light on the different sciences, making them more authentic, closer to the truth. We are still at the beginning of this experience, but the scholars who are part of the Abba School and who are experts in the different subject matters are beginning to experience this in themselves. The articles they write, their lectures, their books bear witness to this.

> —Chiara Lubich at the conferral of an honorary doctorate by the University of Buenos Aires UBA, "The Unity of the Whole Human Family," Buenos Aires, April 6, 1998, published in *Dottorati honoris causa conferiti a Chiara Lubich* (Rome: Città Nuova, 2016), 183–84. Official translation by the Focolare Communication Office/Linguistic Services (COM-SL).

Bibliography

Sources

Archivio Generale Movimento Focolare (AGMF). http://www.focolare.org/chi-siamo/archivio-generale/

Catalano, Roberto. *The Pact: The Spiritual Friendship between Chiara Lubich and Imam W. D. Mohammed.* Hyde Park, NY: New City Press, 2024.

Chiara Badano Foundation. *"In My Staying Is Your Going": The Life and Thoughts of Chiara Luce Badano.* Hyde Park, NY: New City Press, 2021.

Gentilini, Maurizio. *Chiara Lubich: Prophet of Unity.* Hyde Park, NY: New City Press, 2020.

James, Michael, Thomas Masters, and Amy Uelmen. *Education's Highest Aim: Teaching and Learning through a Spirituality of Communion.* Hyde Park, NY: New City Press, 2010.

Lubich, Chiara. *Amatevi come io ho amato voi.* Rome: Città Nuova, 2012.

—— *Attualità: Leggere il proprio tempo.* Edited by Michele Zanzucchi. Rome: Città Nuova Editrice, 2013.

—— *Colloqui con i gen 1970–74.* Rome: Città Nuova, 1999.

—— *The Cry of Jesus Crucified and Forsaken.* Hyde Park, NY: New City Press, 2001.

—— *Essential Writings: Spirituality, Dialogue, Culture.* Hyde Park, NY: New City Press, 2007.

—— *The Eucharist.* Hyde Park, NY: New City Press, 2005.

―― *The Holy Spirit: Renewing the Face of the Earth*. Edited by Florence Gillet and Raul Silva. Hyde Park, NY: New City Press, 2018.
―― *Meditations*. Hyde Park, NY: New City Press, 2023.
―― *A New Way: The Spirituality of Unity*. Hyde Park, NY: New City Press, 2006.
―― *Paradise '49*. Unpublished document. Translated by Thomas Masters and Callan Slipper.
Masters, Thomas, and Amy Uelmen. *Focolare: Living a Spirituality of Unity in the United States*. Hyde Park, NY: New City Press, 2011.
Mitchell, Donald, ed. *Paradise: Reflections on Chiara Lubich's Mystical Journey*. Hyde Park, NY: New City Press, 2020.
Pochet, Michel. *Stars and Tears: A Conversation with Chiara Lubich*. London: New City Press, 1985.
Torno, Armando. *Chiara Lubich: A Biography*. Hyde Park, NY: New City Press, 2012.

For Further Reading

To explore more about Chiara Lubich, the Focolare charism, and the Focolare Movement, readers may wish to consult the following sources:

Books by Chiara Lubich

- *The Art of Loving: A Handbook to Answer the Call of Love*. Hyde Park, NY: New City Press, 2010.
- *The Cry of Jesus Crucified and Forsaken: Finding Light in the Face of Darkness*. Hyde Park, NY: New City Press, 2021.
- *Early Letters: At the Origins of a New Spirituality*. Hyde Park, NY: New City Press, 2015.
- *The Eucharist: Reflections on the Eucharistic Mystery*. Hyde Park, NY: New City Press, 2005.

- *May They All Be One: Origins and Life of the Focolare Movement.* Hyde Park, NY: New City Press, 2023.
- *Meditations.* Hyde Park, NY: New City Press, 2024.
- *A New Way: The Spirituality of Unity.* Hyde Park, NY: New City Press, 2006.

Thematic Collections of Works by Chiara Lubich, with Commentary

- Blaumeiser, Hubertus, ed. *Jesus Forsaken.* Hyde Park, NY: New City Press, 2016.
- Falmi, Donato, and Florence Gillet, eds. *Unity.* New City Press, 2015.
- Falmi Donato, and Judith Povilus, eds. *Jesus in Our Midst: Source of Joy and Light.* Hyde Park, NY: New City Press, 2019.
- Gillet, Florence, and Raul Silva, eds. *The Holy Spirit: Renewing the Face of the Earth.* Hyde Park, NY: New City Press, 2018.
- Leahy, Brendan, and Hubertus Blaumeiser, eds. *The Church: What Is It? Who Is It?* Hyde Park, NY: New City Press, 2019.
- Leahy, Brendan, and Judith Povilus, eds. *Mary: Her Identity, Our Identity.* Hyde Park, NY: New City Press, 2018.
- Masters, Thomas, and Callan Slipper, eds. *Essential Writings: Spirituality, Dialogue, Culture.* Hyde Park, NY: New City Press, 2007.

Exploration of Chiara Lubich and the Focolare Charism

- Cerini, Marisa. *God Who Is Love in the Experience and Thought of Chiara Lubich.* Hyde Park, NY: New City Press, 1992.

- Gillet, Florence. *The Choice of Jesus Forsaken in the Theological Perspective of Chiara Lubich.* Hyde Park, NY: New City Press, 2015.
- Mitchell, Donald, ed. *Paradise: Reflections on Chiara Lubich's Mystical Journey.* Hyde Park, NY: New City Press, 2020.
- Tobler, Stefan, and Judith Povilus, eds. *What Is Unity? A View from Chiara Lubich's Paradise '49.* Hyde Park, NY: New City Press, 2023.

Biographies

- Gallager, Jim. *Chiara Lubich: A Woman's Work.* Hyde Park, NY: New City Press, 1998.
- Gentilini, Maurizio. *Chiara Lubich: Prophet of Unity.* Hyde Park, NY: New City Press, 2020.
- Pochet, Michel. *Stars and Tears: A Conversation with Chiara Lubich.* London: New City, 1985.
- Torno, Armando. *Chiara Lubich: A Biography.* Hyde Park, NY: New City Press, 2012.

Film Biography

- *Chiara Lubich: Love Conquers All.* Directed by Giacomo Campiotti, 2021.

The Focolare Movement

- Lubich, Chiara, Piero Coda, Gerard Rosse, et al. *An Introduction of the Abba School: Conversations from the Focolare's Interdisciplinary Study Center.* Hyde Park, NY: New City Press, 2002.
- Masters, Thomas, and Amy Uelmen. *Focolare: Living a Spirituality of Unity in the United States.* Hyde Park, NY: New City Press, 2011.

Online Resources

- The Focolare Movement's international website, available in several languages: focolare.org.
- The Focolare Movement's North American website: focolare.us.
- The Focolare Movement's publishing entity, including the New City Press bookstore, *Living City* magazine, and various media sources: focolaremedia.com.